SEP 2012

"This book is a must-read for those wanting to find freedom from the lies they've believed. In an honest, hilarious, and timely way, Ketric Newell gives us all a sort of gut check, challenging us to face our junk so we can become all God desires us to be."

—PETE WILSON, senior pastor, Cross Point Church, Nashville; author of *Plan B* and *Empty Promises*

"Only someone with a permed mullet like Ketric Newell could write a book called *Liar, Liar, Mullet On Fire*. I encourage everyone—young or old—to pick up a copy. Laugh and learn along with the mullet man as he discovers the lies we believe and the truth that will set us free!"

—RENEE FISHER, spirited speaker and writer to twentysomethings; author of *Faithbook of Jesus* and *Not Another Dating Book*

"This book is hilarious and powerful. It pulls no punches. If you are a teen looking for a way to discover your true potential, you must read *Liar, Liar, Mullet On Fire*!"

—JOSH SHIPP, author of *The Teen's Guide to World Domination*; host of *Jump Shipp*

LIAR LIAR
Mullet On Fire

Extinguishing Lies We Believe with God's Truth

KETRIC NEWELL

TH1NK, an
Imprint of
NavPress

NAVPRESS
Discipleship Inside Out™

NavPress is the publishing ministry of The Navigators, an international Christian organization and leader in personal spiritual development. NavPress is committed to helping people grow spiritually and enjoy lives of meaning and hope through personal and group resources that are biblically rooted, culturally relevant, and highly practical.

For a free catalog go to www.NavPress.com or call 1.800.366.7788 in the United States or 1.800.839.4769 in Canada.

ISBN-13: 978-1-61747-897-0

Cover design by Arvid Wallen

Some of the anecdotal illustrations in this book are true to life and are included with the permission of the persons involved. All other illustrations are composites of real situations, and any resemblance to people living or dead is coincidental.

Newell, Ketric.
  Liar, liar, mullet on fire : extinguishing lies we believe with God's truth / Ketric Newell.
    p. cm.
  Includes bibliographical references (p.   ).
  ISBN 978-1-61747-897-0
  1. Teenagers—Religious life. 2. Youth—Religious life. 3. Truth—Religious aspects—Christianity I. Title.
  BV4531.3.N49 2012
  248.8'3—dc23

                            2011045863

Printed in the United States of America

1 2 3 4 5 6 7 8 / 17 16 15 14 13 12

Contents

Acknowledgments

THANK YOU TO my beautiful wife, Ashley, for always loving me and being my number one fan.

Thank you, Mom and Dad, for believing in me and always standing behind me.

Thanks to my brother, Kenny, for teaching me how to utilize my imagination.

To my sister, Keista, thank you for being an amazing example for me growing up.

Many thanks to the numerous people who have made an investment in my life.

Thank you, NavPress, for partnering with me on this project and believing in what God has placed on my heart to share.

Introduction

HEY, Y'ALL!

(Yes, I'm an Okie.)

If you're picking up this book right now, it probably means one of four things:

1. You're curious, wondering who the awesome guy in the mullet is. (This is, of course, the most likely option.)

2. You had a mullet in the past, or you have a mullet now, or you're seriously considering getting one. (If you are considering this unique yet stylish trend, please read this book in its entirety before making the cut.) We mullet heads gotta stick together, you know.

3. Your crazy Aunt Rosa (you know the one: the aunt who gives those long, drawn-out, full-frontal hugs and wet kisses, who gives you cheesy gifts for birthdays and Christmases) thought the photo on the front of this book was a photo of you in elementary school and bought a copy for you. (Um, and if you're a girl, that's even weirder.)

4. Finally, maybe you just are *that* cool of a person and you picked up this book on your own. If so, I thank you because I'm trying to find a way to feed my wife and two dogs!

First, let's get the name thing out of the way. *Ketric*. It's not really the sort of name you'd find on the Most Popular Baby Names list, or even one you'd find in a 10,000 Baby Names book, for that matter. It's one of the first things people notice about me. The not-so-polite people will make lame name jokes, and the polite ones will ask where the name came from. Assuming you're the latter, I'm gonna tell you.

When my mom was helping my brother, Kenny, with his math homework, she came across the word *metric*. She liked the word, but she also loved names that start with the letter *K*. (My siblings and I all have *K* names.) So she just changed the *m* of *metric* to a *k* and—*voila!*—*Ketric* was born. Growing up, I heard every incarnation of that word: Patrick, Kedrick, and I even had a substitute teacher call me Katreese. Gotta give that one points for trying! But the name that has stuck with me the most is Ketchup, and I must say, I don't mind it. There are worse nicknames. If you're thinking my last name, *Newell*, is weird too—well, that one's my dad's fault.

Now that we've got *that* out of the way, let me tell you how I got here. I've always had a heart to share with others what I was learning in the Bible as I stumbled through my walk of faith. Even at a young age, I started speaking at camps and churches. When I was in high school, my graduating class of 432 people voted for me to give a speech at graduation, so on graduation day, I stood in front of two thousand people and was able to share what God had done in my life. When I went to college, I started volunteering at LifeChurch.tv with their youth program. And after about three years of serving the youth group, I was asked to pray about coming onto staff at LifeChurch.

Wow, that all sounds pretty straight and simple, doesn't it? But I assure you, as the path unfolded, it was anything but. Even the day they asked me to think about becoming a staff member, I wasn't so sure.

I remember that it was the seventh of August, and for the past eight months, I had been helping my dad with his work because he had been battling cancer. My dad sold Little Debbie cakes. Oh yeah, you know the ones. And while the job definitely had its fringe benefits, I was really more afraid of abandoning my dad.

Plus, I always felt that I would work *with* churches, but I never imagined myself actually working *for* a church (especially not as a pastor). Plus, this was just coming at a bad time. So on August 7, when they asked me to consider a staff position at LifeChurch, I drove about two miles from LifeChurch to a Starbucks, and on the way, I just prayed, "God, if you want me to do this, I just need to know that my job with Dad is completely done and that I don't have anything more to finish and that you're going to take care of him."

When I got to Starbucks and opened my daily devotional to August 7, the heading of that page said, "Now!" And the verse that followed was Matthew 8:21: "'Lord,' another of His disciples said, 'first let me go bury my father'" (HCSB). As I continued to read, the words of the devotional said, "One man wanted to wait until his father died before going with Jesus. This would be an honorable delay. . . . Yet God knew this man, and He knew the man's father. God would have taken care of the man's father, if he only would have followed Jesus."[1]

My jaw dropped. And the devo continued.

"Some opportunities to serve Him, if not accepted immediately, will be lost. Occasions to minister to others may pass us by. . . . The time to respond is *now*."[2]

In that moment, I thought, *Seriously, God?* The sign couldn't have been clearer.

I immediately called my mom and dad and told them everything that had happened, including what I'd just read. They were both so excited for me. "Do it!" they said.

The next day, I started the interview process with LifeChurch.tv, and a week and a half later, I had the job! I was youth pastor at LifeChurch.tv for five years. During that time, I met my to-be-wife, Ashley; had two dogs out of wedlock; and got married. In November 2010 we moved to Nashville, Tennessee, to work with CrossPoint.tv's youth group.

All that to say, even after years in ministry, I'm still not "Pastor" Ketric. Having a title, being a pastor or a president or anything else, doesn't really mean anything. It doesn't mean that we've got all the answers figured out or we don't struggle with issues anymore. God sees just us — plain and simple, who we are — and doesn't worry about our titles.

More than anything, my goal is to let people know — through my ministry, through this book — that it's okay to struggle with problems, battle desires, and get lost in all of the many issues the world dangles in front of us. It's okay because Christ is the way out. He has given us a way to recognize the lies we believe, replace the lies with God's truth, and continue to resist the Enemy in our lives.

You can be free from any addiction, any struggle. And my life, my story (which I'll share with you over the course of this book), proves that. I've been to the gates of hell and back. I've been lied to, tempted, enticed, and tricked. But along the way, I've learned a lot about how those lies, temptations, enticements, and tricks work and how to avoid them. It's not easy. Temptation cannot be eradicated—not in this world anyway. But you can walk along the path lit by the wisdom and truth of God. And let me tell you, the Enemy doesn't like the well-lit path.

It is my hope that by hearing my story, understanding where I came from, and discovering the truths that God has shared with me, you will be able to walk in a freedom that you have never before experienced in your life. I also hope this book makes you laugh while challenging you to break free from the opinions—both yours and others'—that sometimes dominate your life.

Only by replacing the lies of the world with God's truth will you be free!

To freedom!

—Ketric (or Ketchup, whatever)

Operation Code Brown

OKAY, SO LET me tell you a little bit about my life story. And let's start from the very beginning: My mother went to get her tubes tied on a Thursday, and they found me in there.

Some of you reading this book right now don't know what it means to get your tubes tied. Well, I'm not going to explain it to you, but what I want you to do is set down this book, grab a video camera, and walk into the kitchen, living room, or wherever one of your family members may be. Look the person in the face, tilt your head, and say, "What does it mean to get your tubes tied?" Once you capture that on video, send it to me here: Ketric@Ketric.tv. Why? Because I like to laugh!

Okay, so that's not a very good way to start off a story, and it's not a very good way to start off my life, being an accident and all. Although my mom never called me an accident — I was a "surprise." Still, that's not the best self-esteem booster, but hey, writing this book is cheaper than counseling. Now, don't go around feeling sorry for me. That's not how I roll. I would even venture to say that probably half of the baby population was a "surprise."

But back to the point. Not only was I a surprise, I also wasn't normal. Normal babies are born at nine months; I was born at six. Normal babies weigh, say, six to nine pounds; I weighed a little over two. When I was in my mom's belly, I must have overheard the doctor and my mother talking about getting her tubes tied, and it spooked me, so I decided that I had to get out of there as quickly as possible! (The doctor explained it a little differently, but I like my story better.)

Now, since I was born three months early, the hospital had to put me in this warm plastic box called an incubator. I'm not a doctor (I know, shocking, right?), but my technical terminology might overwhelm you. What an incubator does, in technical terms, is . . . well, it cooks you until you are done. So there I was, cooking in an incubator with my little beanie on (along with my little wool socks), loving life, and soaking up the heat. As they continued to examine me, they found something that is called a cranial bleed. Let me explain: *Cranial* refers to a brain, and *bleed* is what blood does. Got it? Okay. So the doctors were going to have to do a little surgery and put what's called a shunt in my head, which would be used to drain the blood off of my brain. But when the doctors went to do the surgery, they couldn't find a single thing wrong! The Lord had healed me right then, three months before I was even supposed to be born! And I've been pretty healthy ever since. I don't have any real big issues today. (All right, some of my friends may argue with that last one. But as we get to know each other, you can just see for yourself.)

One minor issue—or maybe it's more of an incident—came about when I was in the first grade. Back then, I had a haircut called a mullet. I assume you're familiar with the term. You know, "business in the front, party in the back" and all that. I started growing it in the first grade, but I didn't cut it until the fifth grade. That's dedication, my friends.

As if the whole mullet thing weren't interesting enough, mine wasn't just any mullet—it was a *permed* mullet. That's right: My mother permed my mullet in the first grade. (Thanks, Mom!) Needless to say, Mom and I were on the forefront of hair trends. And that permed mullet was just *one* of the notable things about my first-grade year.

Yes, there's more.

Until I was in eighth grade, we lived in the bustling town of Woodward, Oklahoma, and all through elementary school, one of my favorite things was recess. I, of course, thought it was an actual subject, and if it had been, I would've definitely gotten an A++ with a pristine attendance record.

But back to the first grade.

Recess Rules!

I remember the story like it was yesterday. One fine day, that beautiful bell rang and it was time for recess. Ah, recess. Recess was better than anything. It was better than milk breaks or story time. It was better than eating glue (and I ate a lot of glue).

On this particular day, me and my best friend, David Bates, were racing. We were going as fast as we could to get to the holy grail of the playground: the swings. I remember walking down the hall, barely able to contain myself. My brain wanted to move way faster than my body, but I knew that there was no running in the halls, so I started doing the speed walk toward the end of the hallway. You know the one: like your legs are running a forty-yard dash but your upper body is relaxing in a recliner. It was more of a stop-and-go type of movement. You slow down when a teacher walks by but speed up as soon as she's not looking, trying not to make it obvious that you're doing a full-on run. Sure, it makes you look really goofy, but it's effective in a desperate situation.

So we were speed walking down the tiled hallway, past the lockers to our left and right, and we got to the glorious red glow of the illuminated exit sign. Under the sign was that big, heavy, metal door with a long shiny bar across the front of it. I pushed that spring-loaded bar with the full weight of my whole body, and the huge door granted us access to pure freedom. My face was blasted with heat from the outside, the humidity in the air, and the smell of hot asphalt. David and I were already in a full sprint to beat everyone to the swings.

My meticulously gelled mullet curls flapped gracefully in the wind and slapped the back of my neck as I ran. And I wasn't alone. David also had a mullet, but David's mother didn't perm his mullet like my mom did for me. (I like to think of my mullet as my very own Superman cape—a really wrinkled Superman cape. But I digress.) Our mullets flew together like banners of freedom as David and I busted through clusters of kids who stood between us and the swing set. We ran past the basketball goals, past the merry-go-round, and straight toward those chains and that long rubber seat.

When we finally made our trek across the playground, David and I started swinging, sweat running down our faces. Our swinging became more and more intense, and we soon reached the pinnacle of swing choreography, where we were swinging up and down oppositely, passing each other mid-swing. At the same time, we would reach the top in opposite directions, meet back in the middle, and hit the top again. It was sheer perfection.

Code Brown!

Now, I'll try to explain this next part as best I can. David and I had gotten to a very serious level of swinging. When the swing gets to that highest point and starts to come down, for about half a second, the chains go airborne and loose, and as gravity pulls you down, you come smack back down in your seat with a jolt. You playground masters know what I'm talking about. I so wished that I could be the kid who could flip all the way upside down around the bar and come back down like a real pro. I tried it for many years but could never quite swing all the way around. I was pretty close, though!

So there we are, David and I, at that place where we are swinging intensely, and I get this great idea. With my little blond mullet waving through the air, I begin to explain.

"David," I said.

"Yeah?" he replied.

"DAVIIIID!" I yelled.

"YEEEAAHH?!" he yelled back.

"How 'bout every time that we pass each other, let's FART!"

Now, don't judge me, okay? You have to remember that I was born three months early. It may or may not have affected my brain a little bit, all right? For me, this was a big deal. I mean, really, what first-grade boy wouldn't agree that this was a great idea? Which, it was. (It's not like it was in the middle of a prayer at church or something.) As we swung in perfect harmony, David agreed to my brilliant idea, and I was pumped! David was a very relaxed guy. He didn't get as outwardly excited about things as I did, but he went along with it.

So I said, "All right, on the count of three, let's do it!"

He said, "Okay."

"One . . . two . . . three!"

And off we went, passing gas back and forth as we passed each other back and forth. After a while, I started to become a little agitated because he was getting good at this game. My competitive nature was flaring up.

Now, some of you may think that passing gas is a silly thing to get competitive about. But how many of you are the baby of the family? I am. I have a sister who is five years older than me and a brother who is ten years older. You would think that a ten-years-older brother would baby you, right? Wrong. My brother loved to pick on me. I don't know if your brothers and sisters are the same way, but for my brother, it seemed to be the entire reason for his existence. One of his favorite methods of operation was to drop things on the floor and have me bend down to pick them up. Every time I would fall for it, and every time I'd bend down to pick the things up, he would fart in my face. Argh! It would make me so angry!

So there I am, having one of these same moments with David on the swings. I was getting angry because every time he passed me, he would be able to pass gas. And I, on the other hand—well, let's just say that my tank was low. About the fifth time, I decided that I had had enough. I wasn't just going to sit there and let David pass gas in my direction without reciprocating the gesture.

I thought to myself on the swings, *I'm about to drop the hammer on David! I'm going to win this thing, and he's going to fall out of the swing! I'm going to be in the school newspaper, be the coolest kid in school!* I prepared myself and reared back.

As I came down, I tried to unload my arsenal of tear gas on David. However, what I thought was supposed to be gas turned out to be a lot more than just air! In technical terms, you might call it a Code Brown.

My tactic had changed the game all right: It brought my swinging to an immediate halt. I twisted my body around in disbelief to check for evidence. Yep, definitely a Code Brown! In an attempt to win this silly game, I had just pooped my pants, swinging on the swings, in first grade, with a permed mullet.

Even as a young boy, I knew I was in one big mess.

Admit Your Mess

Believe it or not, this disgusting story has a point. Whether we're six or sixty, we all get into messes, don't we? And throughout our lives, we all have the same two choices that I had at that very moment. As I sat there in the swings, there were two things I could've done: choose to sit there in the mess I was in, acting like everything was okay, or deal with it.

I could've gone to my next class after recess and played it off as if everything was fine and normal. I could've acted cool. I could've faked it. (Unless I was called up to the board to do a math problem — then I would've had to say, "I got a problem for you right here in the bottom of my pants!")

But somehow, in all of my six years of wisdom, I chose to deal with it.

I turned to David and told him what I had done. David took my hand and we walked back past the merry-go-round, past the basketball hoops, and up to the door with the glowing exit sign. We walked down that tiled hallway, we passed the lockers on both sides, and we went into the office to tell the secretary that I needed to make a phone call.

The lady behind the desk was a little jumpy. She had gulped her two pots of coffee for the day, and boy was she pumped to be there. Her first question to me was "Why do you need to call your mother?"

That was all it took. Right then, I broke down and cried. In the middle of my tears and snorts and sniffles, all I could muster was one word: "poopie."

At that point, I think she got the hint. She ceased to ask any more questions. She just called my mom.

I remember how long it took to walk across the hot asphalt, down the hallway, and into the office. I felt as if it took forever. I remember how scared I was to tell anyone — even my best friend, David, and definitely the jumpy lady behind the desk — what had happened. But once I had made that phone call, it felt like my mom was there in no time.

When my mom walked into the office, I cautiously looked up at her, feeling dirty, shameful, and embarrassed, and for the first time, I wondered what my mom thought of me. She had always loved me and taken care of me no matter what, but now . . . well, now she knew what a mess I was. She knew everything that had happened. In that moment, I wondered what she thought, and I began to doubt her love for me.

But that didn't last long. When I ran to my mom, she ran to me. I remember bawling as she hugged me. My mother's hug after recess was no different than the hug she gave me that morning when I left. Even though my circumstances — the condition of my underwear, in particular — had changed, her love for me hadn't changed one bit.

I later realized that the way my mom treated me that day was a great picture of the way Jesus treats us when we find ourselves in a mess. The Bible says it like this:

> When God, our kind and loving Savior God, stepped in, he saved us from all that. It was all his doing; we had nothing to do with it. He gave us a good bath, and we came out of it new people, washed inside and out by the Holy Spirit. Our Savior Jesus poured out new life so generously. God's gift has restored our relationship with him and given us back our lives. (Titus 3:4-7, MSG)

That is exactly what my mother did for me when she came and gave me new, clean underwear. It may sound like an odd comparison, but that day my mom gave me back the life I had a few moments before I had gotten myself into a horrible mess.

I know and believe that is exactly what God wants to do through your life and through mine. As long as we will be open and honest, sharing with God where we are and what messes we have found ourselves in, he will always be faithful, even in our unfaithfulness. He is the most consistent thing in your inconsistent life. You have a responsibility, though. He will never force you to be honest with him. You have to *choose* to be honest with him.

So will you? Will you be open with where you are in your life? All of us, at one time or another, will find ourselves in messes that we can't get ourselves out of. In those moments, we have a choice to either sit there in the mess we're in, afraid and ashamed to tell anyone, or get honest and open and allow God to heal us.

As you read this book, do not allow this to just be another notch in your belt, another mark on your checklist, or a simple good read and forget the truth you've heard by tomorrow. Choose to allow the Lord to work in your heart and let these chapters be an active thing in your life that you allow to push you to make the decisions that you know you need to make. Choose to face your fear and expose those things Satan tells you are shameful. His goal is to isolate you and make you feel like you can never tell anybody about your struggles. Why? Because even Satan knows the true and healing power of confessing to one another.

In this next chapter, we are going to talk about the lies that all of us have found ourselves believing when we're right in the middle of our mess. There is a lie that the Enemy is trying to get us to believe. We'll discuss what some of those lies are and how the Enemy gets to us and speaks lies to us. My prayer for you is that you will choose to be bold and tell somebody the mess you are in. Once you confess, as James 5:16 promises, you will find healing.

Tell the Truth

1. Have you ever found yourself in a big mess? What was it? What were the circumstances surrounding the situation?

2. Have you ever shared that mess with anyone?

3. If so, how did that person react? Did sharing the mess with someone else result in a resolution?

4. Do you have or secretly want a mullet? (Come on, tell the truth!)

Origin of the Lie

SO WHAT HAPPENS when we find ourselves in a mess? What happens when we've done something that we know we shouldn't or when we're in a situation that we know we should get out of?

One thing is for sure: The Enemy knows we're vulnerable and goes to work.

That's when the lies begin.

Lies are *always* being thrown at us, if you think about it. They may stem from thoughts or things we've said about ourselves, they may be a result of certain circumstances in our lives, or they may come from things our parents or friends or teachers have spoken to us. They may come from what someone has done to us. It doesn't really matter where they come from. At some point in life, all of us come to a place where we allow the truth to be replaced with a lie. And when that happens, something gets stolen from us.

It's simply the way the Enemy works. John 10:10 tells us, "The thief comes only to steal and kill and destroy; I have come that they may have life, and have it to the full." The Bible calls the Enemy the "father of lies" (John 8:44) for a reason.

There's only one being out there who is trying to feed you lies and get you to believe them. There is only one who is stealing from, killing, and destroying us. And it's not God.

The Sheep, the Coin, and the Son

In Luke 15, Jesus teaches with three different parables. The first one is about a lost sheep. I'm guessing this lost sheep was going along in his normal day, and as he went, he actually was so consumed with what he was doing that he didn't even know he was lost. Then one day, he looked up and realized he was lost.

Some of you are there. Right now. You didn't even realize that you're lost. You just stumbled across this book because someone told you about it. But right now, reading about that lost sheep, you're beginning to realize that maybe you're lost too. You're still trying to figure out what life's about. You keep asking, *Why in the world have I been put on this earth?* You just go along through your daily life, doing your normal thing. You feel like there is something more to life, but you don't know what it is. And right here in this moment, you're looking up, you've lost your bearings, and you're finally admitting, *Boy, am I lost.*

Or maybe you're more like the lost coin that Jesus talks about in Luke 15. What happens in this parable is this lady, she has ten coins and she loses one of them. They were in her possession. It was her job to take care of them, it was her job to protect them, but somewhere along the way, one of those ten coins got lost. Some of you are like that one coin. It's not really your fault that you're in a mess. It's not your fault that you believed certain lies. You have family members or other trusted leaders who are like this lady, and that family member or teacher or friend was supposed to take care of you and look after you. Somewhere along the way, you got lost because *someone else* didn't make the right choices. Maybe you were abandoned or abused or criticized or ridiculed by someone who was supposed to care for you, and that's the mess you're in. You are living and believing the lie not because of something you did but because of something that was done to you. You are a little lost coin just hoping to be found again.

Then there's the third parable about the lost son, found in Luke 15:11-20:

> There was a man who had two sons. The younger one said to his father, "Father, give me my share of the estate." So he divided his property between them.
>
> Not long after that, the younger son got together all he had, set off for a distant country and there squandered his wealth in wild living. After he had spent everything, there was a severe famine in that whole country, and he began to be in need. So he went and hired himself out to a citizen of that country, who sent him to his fields to feed the pigs. He longed to fill his stomach with the pods that the pigs were eating, but no one gave him anything.
>
> When he came to his senses, he said, "How many of my father's hired servants have food to spare, and here I am starving to death! I will set out and go back to my father and say to him: Father, I have sinned against heaven and against you. I am no longer worthy to be called your son; make me like one of your hired servants." So he got up and went to his father.

This son was raised in a good family, with everything that he needed, and knew the right things that he needed to do. But at some point, he just decided that maybe what his parents believed and how they raised him just wasn't true, so he set out to do his own thing. And that's when the mess began.

This is exactly where some of you are. You are in a mess not because of what someone else has done but because of your own choices. It is all because somewhere along the way, you believed the lie that you were better off doing your own thing, apart from rules, apart from parents. (Honestly, I think that nature is in most of us.) If you're here, trust me, it's okay. I'm gonna show you the way back to the truth.

Jesus purposefully shared those three tales of the lost:

- The sheep who didn't know he was lost
- The coin, neglected by its guardian
- The son, who knew better but did it anyway

The sheep, the coin, the son — we could all fit into one of these three situations, couldn't we? If you can see yourself in one of these three parables, you will begin to discover the origin of the lie in your own life.

The Original Lie

We can trace it back even further, back to where it all started, when the first created man and woman lived and existed together, and where the very first lie was told. It's an all-too-clear example of how the Enemy replaced the gift of God's truth with the disastrous lie he was trying to feed them.

Let's pick up the story in Genesis 3:1. "The serpent was more crafty than any of the wild animals the LORD God had made. He said to the woman, 'Did God really say, "You must not eat from any tree in the garden"?'" Do you see it? Right there in the middle of the story, the serpent Satan tries to get Eve to doubt what God had spoken to her, ultimately trying to get her to doubt her Creator.

Why would she even consider such a thing? Adam and Eve had the infinite bounty of the Garden of Eden; they had the most beautiful place on earth to do with what they pleased. What more could they ask for? But Satan has a way of showing us what we don't have, doesn't he? Satan taunted Eve with the *only* area God had forbidden. With his clever M.O.—to steal, kill, and destroy—Satan coaxed Eve's mindset away from the abundance she did have. Then he magnified and focused her gaze on the one thing she didn't have. He did everything he could to convince Eve that God was holding out on her and her garden-mate, Adam.

You've gotta give the girl some credit. She didn't give in without a fight. She told that serpent in verse 3, "God did say, 'You must not eat fruit from the tree that is in the middle of the garden, and you must not touch it, or you will die.'"

The serpent is quick to retort, never even giving Eve a chance to think. In verse 4, "'You will not certainly die,' the serpent said to the woman. 'For God knows that when you eat from it your eyes will be opened, and you will be like God, knowing good and evil.'"

Satan's reply has a familiar ring to it, huh? "What?! It's not like you're gonna die if you stay out after midnight! Your parents just don't want you to have any fun." The serpent is just one of the many forms the Enemy can take on.

So the serpent and Eve are going back and forth. Eve is trying to tell the serpent the truth that God has spoken to her, and the serpent is trying to get her to stop believing the truth she has heard and get her to start believing what he is saying.

Rewriting Eve

Let's stop right here. We all know the end of the story, don't we? We all know that Eve caves, then pulls Adam down with her. But let's forget all of that for a moment. Just for the sake of example, let's write a different ending for Eve.

What if Eve hadn't given in?

Suppose for a moment that Genesis 3:6 read like this: "Eve squared her shoulders and said, 'Listen here, you slithering snake, I'm not sure why you think I'd believe a beady-eyed nobody like yourself! Let me introduce you to my God. That's right: My God is Creator of the entire universe, and if he says don't eat from the tree, then, buddy, I ain't eatin' from no tree!'" (And then, if she were a girl from Oklahoma, she'd take an ax to the head of that old serpent. But that part's optional, I guess.)

If you had just read *that*, closed your Bible, and looked around, what would this world look like? How would it be different?

Difficult to fathom, isn't it?

If Eve were the role model of resisting, if the Fall hadn't happened that day, would there be disease, destruction, death? Would we all be living in our Gardens of Eden, footloose and sin-free?

What about you? What lie do you need to put in its place today? What are *you* believing that is just not true? In your own life, can you remember the origin of that lie? Would you recall the moment when you first started to believe something about yourself that wasn't true?

Someone you deeply loved left you.

"You are unlovable."

You surprised Mom by cleaning the house, and all she did was point out the places you missed.

"You can never be good enough."

You compared yourself with the perfectly shaped women from magazines or school.

"You'll always be ugly."

Are you *there*? Is the lie slowly beginning to reveal itself? Do you remember the day the lie was introduced, the moment the serpent first spoke to you, trying to make you doubt your Creator?

Good. Hang on to that scene for a bit. It may be painful, it may be embarrassing, it may be hard to remember. But together, you and I are going to rewrite the script of that day—and every day from here on out.

(Again, the ax is optional.)

Tell the Truth

1. Jesus spoke of the sheep, the coin, and the son. Which story best fits your situation?

2. Think back to a time when lies were whispered or truths were twisted. How did the story go?

3. If you could rewrite that story, what would be different? What would you say? What would you do?

Living the Lie

ONE OF MY pastors used to always say that if you believe a lie as if it were true, it will begin to affect your life as if it is true. I love that! Read it again: If you believe a lie as if it were true, it will begin to affect your life as if it is true. So what do I mean by that?

The Santa Claus Conspiracy

Let me explain it this way. Think about Santa Claus. Isn't it a really crazy story? For most people (at least around here), somewhere in your life, your family told you that a big, white-haired, bushy-faced man is going to sneak into your house on Christmas Eve while you are sleeping. He'll eat your food, drink your milk, snoop around, and then leave you presents.

And you will be okay with that.

(At the same time, you're being taught not to take gifts from strangers.)

You and I are okay with some creepy guy breaking into our home in the middle of the night and eating our food while we're sleeping? Really? Since *when*? Is there *any* other situation where *anyone* would *ever* be okay with that? And the crazier thing about the story is that everyone around us is in on it: our own family members, moviemakers, authors, people at the mall.

The mall hires some guy to come sit in the chair for twelve hours a day, holding wiggly, screaming kids, while Mom pays astronomical amounts for bad photos of her precious children sitting in a stranger's lap! They're paying all kinds of money for this sort of thing—for a lie. Kids are even encouraged by everyone to believe that the mall Santa Claus is the real Santa Claus, when the "real" Santa Claus doesn't even exist! (Sorry, I broke the news. Someone's gotta be honest here.) And that's not to mention the money spent on producing and seeing Santa movies and making and buying Santa books, blow-up Santas, tacky Santa figurines, Santa costumes. The list goes on and on.

Here's the kicker to the story: Most of the people promoting the Santa Claus story had that same story passed down to them in their own childhood.

I remember the day my mom and my dad admitted that this whole story about Santa Claus and his eight reindeer flying and landing on my rooftop wasn't true. It made me cry. I bawled my eyes out. Something that I had believed until I was eight years old (or maybe sixteen and a half, or eighteen . . . but whatever) was all one big lie.

Santa Claus is only one illustration of how lies can spread like wildfire in our world, our society, and our lives. Often the lies are passed down to us from our parents, our guardians, or the people around us simply because they were passed on to them by their own parents and people around them. Unfortunately, however, most wildfire lies are much more harmful than a jolly guy bearing gifts.

Feeding the Lie

That statement my pastor made is all too true. I believed the lie, that Santa Claus is real, and it certainly affected my life as if Santa Claus were real.

Like the cookies. Every year on Christmas Eve, my siblings and I had left cookies and milk for the man in the red suit who was planning to break into our house that night. Oh, to count the cookies I'd forfeited over the years — for nothing! I was actively, regularly feeding that lie, quite literally.

We feed all kinds of lies, don't we?

Sure, someone else may create the lie: "Ha! You'll never make the basketball team. You can barely dribble!"

Why is it that we even allow the lie to continue beyond that point? Why do we allow someone else to shape our thinking? But we do. As soon as any negative phrase is uttered, we typically allow it to take root somewhere in our minds. Of course, that negative statement probably isn't even true, but we let it in, almost inviting it to negatively shape our view of ourselves. Maybe the mean words were snapped by a friend who was just having a bad day. Or maybe it was a classmate who was just jealous of your muscular physique. (I, of course, had that problem all the time!) It could have simply been a sarcastic joke. But your doubts, your insecurities, your anxieties — they all hear the lie, pull it in, and hold on tight.

Now, if we were aware of what was taking place — a lie taking root — we *could* just dismiss it. But do we? Nah. And to make matters worse, we feed it.

We think:

Hmmm, maybe he's right. Maybe I shouldn't try out for the team.

There was that one time, when I tripped up the stairs . . .

What if I get out there, with everyone watching, and fall flat on my face?

If I can't play basketball, what can I do?

Man, I'm worthless.

Do you see what happened? A simple spoken word — an *untrue* word, at that — was allowed to settle in to a person's mind, and the mind fed it, treated it as if it were truth.

Whether we feed a lie with cookies or by giving it a nice cozy spot in our brains — agreeing with it, inviting it to stay for a while — feeding our lies changes our lives. And rarely does it change our lives for the better.

Playing the Part

You know what happens next, don't you? Yep. When your mind believes something is true, your actions reflect that truth.

In the basketball example, it wasn't long before one bad remark turned into feelings of worthlessness. And let me tell you, it's all downhill from there. You've probably seen friends (or maybe even yourself) turn poor self-worth into really poor decisions. Cutting, drug and alcohol abuse, and messing around or hooking up with someone can all stem from not valuing yourself enough to take care of yourself. When you start to believe the negative things people say about you, it can affect your life in really negative ways.

And in the Santa Claus Conspiracy, I know you've heard somebody say, "Santa Claus is watching you!" Parents and grandparents use it as a behavioral incentive, a reminder for kids to be good, which is a positive thing, I guess. But it's also a really common example of how a lie is used to manipulate your behavior. And it works.

In fact, it's been working since the beginning of the world. Picking up in Genesis 3:6, we watch Eve agree with the serpent's lie and then act on it: "When the woman saw that the fruit of the tree was good for food and pleasing to the eye, and also desirable for gaining wisdom, she took some and ate it."

It's like watching a scene from a scary movie, isn't it? You're sitting there, watching, knowing the character is about to make a dumb decision — knowing that if Eve takes a bite, she'll die. We're not sure how she'll die, but God has promised death, and she's gonna get it.

Popcorn is flying, and you're screaming at the TV, "NOO, Eve! Don't do it! It's a snake! Can't you see that? Why would you believe a snake over God?!"

Then the plot thickens. "She also gave some to her husband, who was with her, and he ate it" (verse 6).

"You've got to be kidding me!" we scream. "Adam, you're taking advice from someone who listens to snakes! Who wrote this movie anyway?!"

Well, we did.

Humans wrote these ignorant scenes by choosing this stupid, sinful course. We're not God. We don't see all. We certainly don't know all. And we sometimes do really, *really* dumb things, based on really, *really* dumb ideas, given to us by really, *really* dumb people — or, namely, Satan himself.

Adam and Eve were living the absolute perfect life before that sneaky serpent came along. No sin. No shame. Nothing was hindering their relationship with God. But when the serpent comes onto the garden path and begins to speak to Eve, he begins to tell her thoughts that were not her thoughts. And so many times, this is how destructive behavior begins.

You know the crazy thing about it? The only power the Enemy can have over you is the power that you choose to give him. That's right: the power he uses against you is your own. If God doesn't force you to do anything, what makes you think that Satan can? Satan's power is limited to your cooperation with him. That's huge!

When the serpent came into the garden, he didn't force Eve to eat that apple. The only thing he did was convince her to doubt God. He didn't wrap his slimy self around her and say, "You must eat the apple. You have no choice!" That's not what he did. He was sly and crafty. He spoke thoughts to her and swayed her into believing it was a good idea.

At first, Eve was on the right track, rebuking what the Devil was saying and repeating back to him the words of God. But where Eve went wrong is that she did not change her environment. She didn't run from the lies she was hearing. She stayed and continued to allow the thoughts of the Enemy to creep into her mind. Eventually, as the serpent continued to speak to her, she took his words and made them her own thoughts. And from there, her thoughts produced action.

Eve chose to eat the fruit.

Satan couldn't make her.

And he can't make us.

Yup, just like the horror movies, we make the dumb decisions all by ourselves.

Unlike the horror films, thankfully, we real-life characters are offered the gift of redemption. But we first have to realize and admit the mess we're in. And sometimes that can be the most difficult step to take.

Tell the Truth

1. What lies are influencing your behavior?

2. Who are your co-conspirators? Who is trying to sell you a story that just isn't true?

3. So if your life is a horror film, what are the viewers screaming as they watch?

Confronting the Lie

4

WHEN ADAM AND Eve were in a mess, they did what any of us might do: They ran like chickens and hid. (Hiding from God = Not the best plan.)

> Then the man and his wife heard the sound of the LORD God as he was walking in the garden in the cool of the day, and they hid from the LORD God among the trees of the garden. But the LORD God called to the man, "Where are you?" (Genesis 3:8-9)

Where Are You?

Where are you? Now, why would God ask them *that*? Were they playing a game of hide-and-seek? Or did God really not know where they were? Well, here's a hint: God is God. He knows everything. If you play hide-and-seek with God, you are going to lose.

God seemed to be asking that question solely for the benefit of Adam and Eve. He wanted *them* to examine where their decision had led them. He didn't want them to walk around in their own mess and not know it. And he knew that Adam and Eve certainly weren't going to make the effort to clean themselves up if they didn't even realize they were in a mess to start with.

The same is true for us. God will not fix the things in our lives that we choose to ignore. God will not force you to give up something in your life. You have to want to. Right now, as you consider some of the messy situations you're in, I want you to ask yourself, *Do I know where I am? Do I want to quit? Do I want to sit in my mess forever? Or do I truly want freedom?*

I'm only asking because I've been there and I've had to answer that question for myself. There was a time when I was choosing to live a sinful life. I knew that I should have quit my lifestyle, and I really did want to be free of that sin and toxic thinking. But the truth is, I wasn't willing to give up my daily routine and certain things in my life in order to be free. I would sit down with friends or mentors and tell them I was struggling, but truth be told, I wasn't struggling at all. I was just doing it. No part of me was trying to resist. Struggling means you are actively putting elements in place to overcome it. I was straight up choosing to sin.

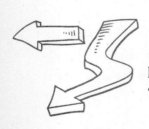

My question to you is: "What is that thing that you need to uncover, expose, and let out?" More important, God is asking, "Where are *you*?"

Taking the Blame

Wait! Don't answer that. Not yet.

First, let me tell you how *not* to answer that question.

Once again, we can take a what-not-to-do cue from our poor friends Adam and Eve. When God (you know, that God-who-knows-everything God) asks Adam and Eve where they are, guess how they respond.

Well, how would *you* respond?

(To the God who knows everything.)

That's right.

Blame it on someone else!

Let's take a look:

GOD: *Adam? Adam, where are you?*

ADAM: *Well, you see, God, I, um, well, I heard you coming, and I was afraid, because, see here, I don't have any clothes on, and well, so — I hid.*

GOD: *Who said you're naked? Adam, did you eat from that tree?*

ADAM: *Weeeeell, do you remember the woman you stuck in the garden with me? She's the one who gave me the fruit. Yeah, she gave it to me. And, I mean, you did put her with me, so I listened to her. Well, what else could I do, really? So yeah, I guess I ate it.*

Okay, so this is from the KVB (you know, the Ketric Version of the Bible), but the real Bible doesn't read much differently. (Seriously. Read it! Genesis 3:9-12.) In the passage, we see the classic Liar Defense Tactics at work:

1. Stall. (Babbling is a definite plus.)
2. Never answer the question directly.
3. And no matter what, in all circumstances, blame it on someone else!

And Adam didn't just blame it on Eve ("But *she* gave it to me!"). Ohhh no. Did you catch what else he did? Oh yeah, he deflected the blame to *God*, too.

When God asked Adam if he ate from the tree, note his response. In verse 12, he said, "The woman you put here with me—she gave me some fruit from the tree, and I ate it." And that one's straight from the Bible! Adam could've simply said, "Yes." Or even, "Yes, I did, God, but I'm sorry." But nooo, he set the example for all liars to follow: "All I did was listen to the woman *you* put here with me!" Adam had some nerve. Or stupidity. I'm not sure which.

When God then turned to Eve, she had already seen the error of Adam's blameful ways. She, no doubt, chose the wiser path. She immediately said, "Yes, God. I ate from the tree, and I'm sorry."

Right?

Wrong.

Eve's response—and I quote—was this: "The serpent deceived me, and I ate" (verse 13).

So Adam pointed to God and Eve. Then Eve pointed to the serpent. The good ol' finger-pointing fiasco.

A simple yes would have sufficed. That's all God needed to hear.

And that's all he needs from you.

God, the First Fashion Designer

After Adam and Eve had confessed their sin (despite how badly they had fumbled the confession), God took action. Although there were consequences from their actions, God didn't stop caring for them. He reached down and helped them move forward.

Of course, Adam and Eve had *attempted* to clean up the mess on their own. The fruit had made them realize they were naked, and Genesis 3:7 tells us that they had covered themselves in fig leaves. Now, imagine for a moment the functional challenges that dressing in fig leaves would cause. First, I doubt that tying fig branches around your waist was very comfortable . . . or secure. Oh, the wardrobe malfunctions that fig branches invite! How do you think they were held in place? A vine belt? And wouldn't you imagine the leaves would dry up every few days? What would they do in the fall, when the fig trees lost their leaves? Branches of pine needles? Yeowch. I'm no fashion expert, but it's pretty obvious that Adam and Eve's solution to their wardrobe challenge wasn't the most efficient one.

Then comes God, the Creator of creativity, the very first fashion designer. In Genesis 3:21, we learn that God covered Adam and Eve in animal skin. Who, but God, would have even thought to do that? I can't speak for Adam and Eve, but

I would certainly prefer the softness of suede to the bristle of fig branches. Wouldn't you?

Plus, do you realize that God had to kill an animal in order to get the animal skin? Have you ever thought about that? This is the first time in the Bible that God sacrificed something for his people and covered them with it. It is a foreshadowing of what Christ, the final sacrifice, did for us. Even when you and I were in the midst of porn, drugs, alcohol, sex, lust, cutting, shame, fear, molestation, abuse, and countless others sins, he came and covered us.

It's worth noting here, too, that God didn't rewind time, even though he could have. He didn't choose to erase the sin or its result. (Adam and Eve were still ashamed; they still knew they were naked.) Nope, our God took Adam and Eve, right there where they were, and helped them begin the process of moving forward.

Loving You, Lies and All

Romans 5:8 says, "While we were still sinners, Christ died for us." Do you see that? While we *were still* sinners. It doesn't take a pastor to tell you that means in the middle of our choosing to disobey God, to do whatever sin we were doing, Jesus Christ made a decision about you. He isn't disillusioned. He doesn't think that maybe you can fix yourself and then come to him. (And if you *do* try to fix yourself—take it from Adam and Eve—the solutions are usually inefficient and short-lived.) He wants you to come to him in the middle of your sin, for the permanent solution: forgiveness.

The Bible says in James 5:16, "Confess your sins to each other and pray for each other so that you may be healed. The prayer of a righteous person is powerful and effective." There's something extremely powerful and freeing about confessing out loud to someone else. It allows what has been in the dark, what you have feared being exposed, to come into the light. When you do that, something spiritual happens. God sends people around you to love you and guide you and help you see that you're not alone. You're not the only one who's dealing with it; there are many who have gone before you.

God knows that you can't do it on your own, and he isn't asking you to. He wants you to answer the same thing: *Where are you? What mess are you covered in?* He is also asking if you will allow him in and uncover the things you are hiding so that he can re-cover you with Christ.

Trust me, there's only one way out.

Confront the lie.

Confess the sin.

And be covered in his infinite grace.

Tell the Truth

1. So *where are you?* What mess are you in the midst of?

2. Who have you been blaming for your mess?

3. Okay, now, who is *really* to blame for the situation you're in?

4. Talk to God about it. You'll find that grace awaits.

Combating the Lie

ONE DAY IN the first grade (hmmm, I'm now thinking that was a bad year), my teacher called me up to the chalkboard. I had my little chalk in hand, and the teacher was asking me to write something on the board. For some reason, after that moment, I remember feeling stupid. To this day, I don't really know what she said that made me feel so intimidated, but all I can tell you is that's when I remember believing my first lie. For years, I believed that I was dumb.

How did I get there? Well, from that day in first grade forward, I would feed that lie:

I'm dumb.
I am not as smart as the other kids.
I can't learn like they learn.
I'm just slower than they are.
I will never be as smart as they are.
I'll always be behind.

The Mind Filter

The thing that you and I have to know if we want to combat the lies coming from all directions is that every thought that comes into our minds is not always our own thought. Nor is it always true. Yes, it's coming at us. Yes, it's hitting us in the face. Yes, we hear it in our heads. But none of that means that every thought rolling around in our heads is truth.

In fact, many of the thoughts are lies. As a people, we've done a horrible job of filtering those thoughts out, and that has got to stop. We've got to choose which thoughts line up with the Word of God, and we have to cast away every single other thought that doesn't. Hebrews 12:1 tells us to "throw off everything that hinders and the sin that so easily entangles."

All of us are telling ourselves assumptions and "facts" about our own lives. Most of us are saying things about ourselves that are simply not true. Some of you say, "I'm addicted, I'm addicted, I'm addicted," so many times that you now believe it to be true. Some of you think that you're not lovable because someone walked out of your life. Some of you think you're dirty because of things you've done. Some of you sabotage success or blessings in your life because you don't feel worthy.

How do I know? The same way I've learned the rest of this stuff: I've been there. From fifth grade all the way into my twenties, I wholeheartedly believed that I was an addict. Yes. In fifth grade. That's when someone very close to me gave me a *Playboy* magazine. That's the day that I was introduced to pornography.

For more than ten years, as a boy and young man, I was struggling with this hidden, dark, lustful life of porn. At first

I told myself that I wasn't addicted, but after a while, as I spent time with my friends and the people around me, I knew that they too struggled with pornography. So I just went along with them. I thought it was every man's battle. I thought that everyone struggled with it. I thought it was just the way I was as a man in this world. I believed that I couldn't ever be free, that it was just my addiction. And from then on, I truly believed that I was addicted to pornography. After telling myself over and over, "I'm addicted, I'm addicted, I'm addicted," I eventually came to believe I could never be free.

Then, in college, I took a trip to Nashville for a large Christian event called the Passion Conference. The speaker was Louie Giglio, and that man said something I will never forget. He read from Colossians 1:27, "To them God has chosen to make known among the Gentiles the glorious riches of this mystery, which is Christ in you, the hope of glory." When I heard Louie speak those words, I fell to my knees in that arena in Nashville.

Finding Freedom

At age twenty-one, I finally realized that I could be free from pornography.

Christ is in me.

I was not addicted. I didn't have to believe that I was going to be stuck in pornography for the rest of my life.

"The hope of glory."

I could be free.

I cried through that entire sermon, and right then I began a journey that led me through all kinds of Scriptures. That's when God began to show me and share with me the truth about his beloved creation: me. God took me to Colossians 3:2-3, which told me, "Set your minds on things above, not on earthly things. For you died, and your life is now hidden with Christ in God." When I read that verse, I finally realized that not only *could* I be free but also that I was *already* free, if I chose to be. The old sinful Ketric was dead; Christ's life was and is living in me. That changed everything. And it taught me that when you really get into the Scriptures, when you begin to believe the One who *made* you (not what everyone else has told you all your life), everything will change.

Romans 10:17 takes that a step further. "Faith comes from hearing the message, and the message is heard through the word about Christ." If you've grown up in or around church, "Faith comes from hearing" is probably a phrase that you're familiar with. But what exactly does that mean for you and me, right here, right now? Well, when it comes to walking in God's truth, it means a whole lot. Basically, whatever you hear, if you hear it enough, eventually you're going to walk it out. Sooo, if you're hearing the truth of God, then you'll eventually walk out the truth of God. Awesome, right? But the converse is true too: If you're listening to the words of the world, you're eventually going to walk with the world.

Do you see how important it is to filter what goes into your brain?! It is quite literally a life-or-death situation.

Draw a picture of Super YOU dressed in full armor. Now post it somewhere or stick it in your wallet to be reminded of God's armor every
day.

Put On Your Armor

God knew it wouldn't be easy for us. He makes it very clear that there's a battle going on here on earth. In Ephesians 6:11-12, we're instructed to "put on the full armor of God, so that you can take your stand against the devil's schemes. For our struggle is not against flesh and blood, but against the rulers, against the authorities, against the powers of this dark world and against the spiritual forces of evil in the heavenly realms."

It's very fitting, too, that when describing this "armor of God," Ephesians begins with the truth: "Stand firm then, with the belt of truth buckled around your waist" (verse 14). And what's the purpose of this armor that we're putting on? "So that when the day of evil comes, you may be able to stand your ground, and after you have done everything, to stand" (verse 13).

See, we try to make our problems, our messes, sound so hopeless and complicated. But we have everything we need to combat the lies around us, and it's been there all along.

God provided the answers we needed long ago. We just have to know where to go for the truth.

Tell the Truth

1. What's the condition of your mind filter? Are you filtering out the trash, only allowing the truth?

2. Is there an addiction or other lie that you long to be free from? What would freedom look like?

3. Read Ephesians 6:10-17. How would your life be different if you put on that armor today and every day?

Lies On Fire!

WHEN I WAS in high school, I drove a 1986 Buick Somerset. This was a sweet car—white with a red ragtop. Not only was this a 1986 Buick Somerset but this was a 1986 Buick Somerset *Limited Edition*. I mean, for a 1986 car, this thing was the top of its class. It even had a digital speedometer. And electric locks. And electric windows.

The thing with the windows, though, is that the motors were going out. To roll them up, I had to push the button with one hand to get them started, and with the other hand, I had to pull the window up. The power window wouldn't really roll up by itself.

As cool as this car was, I need to be honest here: This was actually my grandma's car. And my grandmother smoked. She smoked a lot. She would smoke in this thing, and she would smoke so much that the lining on the ceiling of the car was starting to come loose from the glue. It started to hang down and was all smashed up against her head while she drove.

That's not cool, man.

To have your windows rolled down in the summertime

and to feel all that flapping and to have the car lining whack-
ing you in the head—well, it just doesn't look cool to the
ladies. So I remedied the problem. With straight pins. I stuck
those pins all over the ceiling of my car (Grandma's car, my
car . . . whatever) to keep that lining up there. It was like a
silvery sea of pins. And the really cool thing was that when you
were leaning the seat back, relaxing, and you looked up at the
ceiling, it looked like stars.

Man, that was a sweet ride.

But that's not the point.

Cooking with the Radio

My sophomore year of high school, I decided to put a CD
player in the car. It was a Sony CD player. I learned from my
brother how to do this. (Yes, the same brother who taught me
to be a competitive farter.) He taught me how to pull everything apart, piece all the wiring back together, and fully install
some tunes.

So when we finished installing this CD player in my car,
I had it all working, and I turned on the ignition. When I did
this, there were still certain things that weren't working. Like,
I didn't know how to operate the CD player. I didn't know how
to set the clock. I didn't know how to program the stations.
I didn't know any of that. So I went inside in search of something that most people would automatically go looking for: an
instruction manual.

I walked in my house and looked around, and conveniently
I found the oven manual.

Awesome! A manual for fixing things. I took this oven manual out to my car and sat in front of the CD player. I began to look through that oven manual to see if it would tell me how to fix my car radio. I tried to follow all the instructions, but things just didn't match up. Nothing was working!

The oven manual couldn't show me how to set my CD player clock. It couldn't teach me how to set the radio stations to different programs. It didn't tell me how to change the song or turn up the volume. Why? Because the one who created that CD player was not the one to write the oven manual. The manual to the oven didn't belong with the CD player. It would be crazy for me to think that an oven manual would have had anything to say about that CD player!

Burn the Manuals!

And yet, do you realize that's what we do all the time? When we go to the things and people around us in search of approval or advice, when we allow them to tell us who we are and how we're supposed to function, when we end up getting lost in the broken chaos of other people's opinions, judgments, rules, and ways of life, when we choose *any* of these lies and allow them to rule our lives, we are looking in all the wrong manuals.

People may tell you all the time that you're addicted, that you're ugly, that you're messed up, that you're never going to be worth anything, that there's no good in you — and you might believe them.

But here's the thing: They did not create you. They are not your maker. They don't know you; they don't know what you're created for or what you were put on this earth to do. They don't know your purpose. But Jeremiah 1:5 reminds us that God does: "Before I formed you in the womb I knew [and] approved of you [as My chosen instrument], and before you were born I separated and set you apart, consecrating you; [and] I appointed you as a prophet to the nations" (AMP).

It's ludicrous for me to go to the oven manual and try to figure out how the clock works on my CD player. And it's just as crazy for you and me to try to construct a manual for our own lives from a collection of broken words, half-truths, and flat-out lies that other struggling humans have written. You are not your maker, and they are not your maker. If we don't read the correct manual, we'll never work right; we'll always be broken.

Want to be whole again? Want to reach your God-given potential? Burn those manuals!

That's right. All the lies, the negative words, the doubt, the insecurity, the anxiety—all of those stupid, misguided opinions and instructions you've been told your whole life. Burn 'em. Rip 'em up. Run them through the shredder. Flatten them with a steamroller. Bury them with concrete.

I don't care how you get rid of them.

Just get rid of them.

Now.

Forever.

I'm gonna show you the only manual you and I will ever need.

Your Maker's Manual

Do you know why God gave us the Bible? Second Timothy does:

> Every Scripture is God-breathed (given by His inspiration) and profitable for instruction, for reproof and conviction of sin, for correction of error and discipline in obedience, [and] for training in righteousness (in holy living, in conformity to God's will in thought, purpose, and action),
>
> So that the man of God may be complete and proficient, well fitted and thoroughly equipped for every good work. (3:16-17, AMP)

In this verse, we read the word *correction* and we probably see it as something bad. Like a correction facility. It's a place where people are sent, and all the place does is remind them of why they are in there. But a true correction, like the one mentioned here, helps people see where they have done wrong and then helps them find out how to make it right.

He didn't give us the Bible so that we would read it and then he could love us. God already loved us. God loved us enough to send his son to die for us. He shed his blood for us and took on our sins to be the sin for us so we could take on his life. So, no, we certainly don't read the Bible to get God to love us.

We read the Bible to find out what we have been given. We read the Bible to find out the truth of who we are and what he has made us to be. Then and only then can we live it out. The Bible is a manual for your life. He wrote it for you. This is your manual; this is your guide.

Even though that CD player had all the components it needed to function properly, I didn't have the knowledge of how to make those parts work. Without that knowledge, so many features of my CD player could never be used. In order for me to use my CD player to its fullest potential, I had to go to the manual that was written specifically for that CD player. I needed the manual that could point out the individual parts, show me how each piece worked individually, how they worked together, how to maintain and care for my radio.

Our manufacturer, our maker, wrote about us, all of our features, our maintenance and care, in our very own manual: the Bible, the Word of God. Not only were we made by God, but as Genesis 1:27 tells us, we were also made *in his image*. So wouldn't it make sense to go to the book that *he wrote* for instructions on how to get through this life?

The Bible isn't just a collection of cutesy Bible stories that we learn in Sunday school. (And even those simple stories hold great significance for our lives.) It isn't a list of impossible rules to follow. (Yet our lives would run much more smoothly if we chose to follow those rules.) What the Bible *is* is a living, breathing collection of practical, timely applications for our lives and what's happening in them *right now*.

Seriously.

It tells us how to live. It reminds us that great, God-chosen people mess up. And it assures us that when we do mess up, we have the love and forgiveness of Jesus Christ. I don't know about you, but I need that kind of daily assurance. I need to know that even in the mess I'm sitting in at this very moment,

Jesus is standing there with his hand outstretched, ready to take me in and love me anyway.

But, please, don't take my word for it. Check it out for yourself. You'll see that the Bible truly is the only instruction manual you'll ever need.

Once we've tossed out all those manuals that just won't work, we must replace them with words from the true manual that was written about us. God made you, and he made you with a purpose that only he fully understands. Others may think your buttons are useless or your clock is way off, but there's only one who understands exactly why he made you that way. Stick with the only manual—written by the only maker—that matters, and you'll begin to find that all of your features function exactly how they're supposed to, and with God's guidance, you'll be able to use them to their fullest potential.

Tell the Truth

1. What inappropriate manuals have you been using to guide your life? List them all. Now wad them up and throw them away.

2. What areas of life do you need instruction in? Search a Bible website or concordance for answers on those topics.

3. Do you study your manual regularly? If not, it's a great time to start. Schedule a daily time to read the Bible and stick with it.

All Things New?

WHEN I FIRST gave my life to Christ, I remember someone reading to me 2 Corinthians 5:17: "If anyone is in Christ, the new creation has come: The old has gone, the new is here!"

That verse meant so much to me. I was so excited. There were a lot of things in my life at that time that I wished would just go away. And for a little while, it seemed like they did. The day I gave my life to Christ felt so pure, so true, so permanent. I was truly dedicated to living my life for him. But shortly after I had returned home—to the old familiar places and situations—it seemed as if that old way of thinking began to come back, and I didn't understand why.

I thought the old had gone.

I thought the new was here.

But there I was, staring at my old self again.

What happened?

Body, Soul, and Spirit

Right now, what I want you to do is look at this figure that I drew.

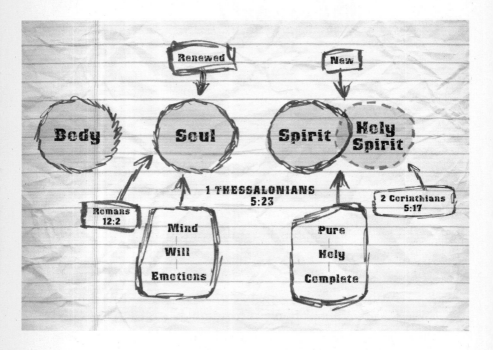

In 1 Thessalonians 5:23, it explains that when you and I come into this world, we are given a body, soul, and spirit. Every single one of us. None of us is exempt from it. These three circles represent each of those things.

The first circle represents your body. Your body is what you get around in. It's what you move. It's what you work out. It's how you pick up the drink from the table. It's what some of you ladies get up and primp and paint with brushes to make it look a certain way. It's your outward appearance.

The second circle represents your soul. Your soul is made up of your mind, will, and emotions. It is where you house everything. Every thought you've ever had, every memory you can contain, every feeling you've ever experienced is stored in your soul. It's kind of like the hard drive on your computer. It's where your personality is found—whether you're an introvert or extrovert, silly or serious. All of this is found in the soul.

The third circle represents your spirit. Connected to the third circle, you'll also find the Holy Spirit. In John 16:7, Jesus said this: "I tell you the truth: It is for your good that I am going away. Unless I go away, the Counselor will not come to you; but if I go, I will send him to you" (NIV, 1984). It is through your spirit that you are able to worship and live in community with God.

You. Are. Holy. (Yes, You.)

The Bible says that the moment you give your life to Christ, your spirit and the Holy Spirit become one. That is when you come into a relationship with God. He takes his Holy Spirit and places it inside you. In 2 Corinthians 5:17, when it says the old is gone and the new is come, your spirit is the "old" and the Holy Spirit is the "new."

The Holy Spirit that you received from Jesus is new, righteous, holy, complete, pure, and finished. It can't get any newer. It can't get any more pure. It is as righteous as it's ever going to be. It is absolutely 100 percent complete and new. Nothing can make it dirty again; nothing can make it incomplete. And that Spirit now lives and resides in you.

Poke your chest.

Right there.

In you.

Holy.

Romans 8 tells us that when we are in Christ, the same Spirit that raised Christ from the dead lives inside us. In fact, it tells us, "If the Spirit of him who raised Jesus from the dead is living in you, he who raised Christ from the dead will also give life to your mortal bodies because of his Spirit who lives in you" (verse 11). If that Spirit is so powerful that it can raise Jesus from the dead, I would say that it can make some pretty powerful transformations in our lives too.

I don't have more of the Holy Spirit because I'm a pastor. Now, I may (or may not) have more Scriptures memorized, and I may (or may not) read and study his Word more, but I don't have any more Jesus than you have. He doesn't withhold anything from any of us.

The moment the Holy Spirit comes to live inside of you, he makes his home there. He doesn't just come for a visit. He makes his home in you, and from that day forward, as we're told in Hebrews 13:5, he will *never* leave you or forsake you.

You know, I used to go into church, and during worship I would pray, *God, I want more of you.* I remember when God began to share with me that I already had all of him; I didn't need to keep asking for more. I got all of him when I received Jesus. In that moment, he came to live in my heart. God then made it very clear that it wasn't that I needed him to come *in* from the outside but that I needed his Spirit to flow *out* of me.

Sure, right now, you may feel that because of your sin, you are unworthy, you are unrighteous, and you are not holy. But that is not the truth. We are righteous. We are complete. We are holy.

A lot of times, we'll hear in church that we are sinners and we're saved over and over by grace. But let's take a look at Romans 5:8. That verse tells us something very different: "God demonstrates his own love for us in this: While we were still sinners, Christ died for us." Did you notice the word *were*? Now, I've made it very clear that I'm no scholar, but I do believe that *were* is a past-tense word. Correct? If I were going to make *were* a present-tense word, making Romans 5:8 a present-tense statement, I would've said, "We *are* still sinners," right? But that's not what this verse is saying, is it? This verse clearly says, "We were still sinners." Past tense. *Were*. Used to be. That is *not* who we *are*.

Everything that Christ has done is in the past tense. He is not *going* to do it; he already has done it. When you received Christ, the moment that you received him, Jesus didn't go right then and die on the cross, did he? Of course not. He died for you two thousand years ago. It was in the moment that you received Christ—five years, five months, or five minutes ago—that you received what he did two thousand years ago. So you and I are not sinners anymore. We were sinners, but we have been saved by grace. You have to get this. You have to understand this. If you don't get this, you will walk around saying, "I'm a sinner. I'm a sinner. I'm a sinner." And when we put that label on ourselves, we just do what we're called to do: We act like sinners.

Transformation is from the inside out. When you and I realize we've been given everything we need through Jesus, we'll stop asking him for it and start living from it.

So right now, I want to share a secret with you. Lean in. Bring your nose closer to this page. *You have all the Jesus you're ever going to need.* You're not going to get any more tomorrow. If you've received Christ into your heart, God has given you everything you need to have a powerful, loving, abundant, peaceful life. The Spirit of God that raised Jesus from the dead now resides in you. It's all there. Not just some of it; every bit of it lives and resides in you.

So stop asking God for it.

It has already been given to you.

If you're still having issues, if you still feel like you're succumbing to the desires of this world, the issue isn't whether you have all the Jesus you need or all the Holy Spirit you need. The moment that Jesus gave you his Spirit, he gave you all of it.

And that's all you're ever going to need.

Transformers

Yeah, I know. That all sounds great, doesn't it? But if we have all that we need, why are we still having issues?

Well for me (and I'm guessing for you, too), the issues that started happening, the feelings that I felt when the old started coming back again, it wasn't a problem with my spirit. It was a problem within my soul. Even though I had a brand-new spirit—a holy one, at that!—my soul was not at all new. Or holy. My soul was still filled with all of the old dusty, holey, imperfect memories, experiences, and feelings I had gathered throughout my life.

When you come to Christ, your soul just *begins* the process of being renewed. That doesn't happen overnight. It takes cooperation and obedience on your part. It is a continual, intentional way of life.

In your instruction manual, Romans 12:2 gives explicit instructions on how to reprogram your mind: "Do not conform to the pattern of this world, but be transformed by the renewing of your mind. Then you will be able to test and approve what God's will is — his good, pleasing and perfect will."

Okay. Now stop. Go back. Read that again.

When I read that verse, I see three direct instructions:

1. Do not conform to what the world does.
2. Renew your mind with God's truth.
3. Use that truth to seek God's will.

Memorize it. Think about it. Apply it. Every day.

It really is that simple. And that difficult.

As a new Christian — honestly, as *any* Christian — this will take some work. I believe that the Christian community does a disservice when we make becoming a Christian sound like a magical, fairy-godmother transformation. Yes, the Holy Spirit comes to help out, but it doesn't take over. You still have the power of free will. You can still choose whether or not to cooperate with the leadings of the Holy Spirit. God knows that in order for you to be truly transformed, a renewing must also occur in the mind, soul, and body.

You can't be a new creature in Christ and still fill your mind with the thoughts of the world. You can't be a new creature in Christ and allow your body to keep doing worldly things. That's why I was so confused; that's where I had gone wrong. I had given my heart to Christ. The Holy Spirit was now at home somewhere inside me. But my body and mind were still going through their same old motions, and I realized that I was the only one who could change that.

We don't become puppets when we become Christians, with God taking control of our strings. We have to choose the things of God and pursue his way of living to continue renewing our soul and live in freedom. Maybe you're having an issue, like I was, and you aren't walking in freedom. It's not that you haven't been given the tools to be free; it's that you haven't yet renewed your mind with the Word of God. When you begin to renew your mind, your soul, with God's truth, you will naturally begin to walk in that freedom and pursue the things of God.

God will dose you with huge helpings of his Spirit.

But your mind is up to you.

Tell the Truth

1. Have you given your life to Christ? If so, did you immediately feel brand new? Are you still trying to get rid of old feelings, habits, and emotions? If you have not given your life to Christ, would you like to? (You'll learn more about how to receive Christ on page 136.)

2. Do you ever hear that little God-like voice speaking to you from your spirit? How do you respond?

3. What steps have you taken to renew your mind?

Finding Truth

OKAY, SO RENEW the mind.

All right.

Sounds good.

But . . .

Um . . .

Just exactly how do I do that?

Well, for starters, you have to remember that every thought that hits your mind is not necessarily yours. The Enemy wants to make you acknowledge the lie, believe the lie, and act on the lie until it becomes your life. It could be the smallest thing from a comment about you to a full-blown addiction you struggle with. And the better you get at recognizing these lies, the sneakier the Enemy gets at telling them to you.

We've talked about some of these lies, and I hope that you have been able to track them to see the effects they have had on your life once you accepted them as truth. Many times, we can look back and see how those lies have made a pivotal difference in who we are.

When I look back at writing on the board in first grade and

feeling like the dumbest kid in the class, I now know that was the beginning of a lie. For years, that lie rolled around in my head like a marble in a paint can. From the third grade to the eighth grade, I was placed in a learning-disability class for reading. I was shamefully set apart from everybody else. At that time, my parents and I didn't dare question the authorities who placed me there. Surely, they knew what they were talking about! The teachers, the principal, the parents—everybody joined in. Nobody questioned their assessment, not even me. We just blindly believed.

Maybe that's not the type of lie you've encountered; maybe yours is closer to the struggle I had with pornography. It was a choice I was making, a way of life I was actively participating in, while believing the lie, "I'm addicted." I chose to see no way out.

I've shared with you the darkest and most secretive lie I've dealt with in my life, and I'm asking you to take that same step of faith. Of course, you don't have to publish it in a book like I am, but on a smaller, but no-less-impactful scale, will you recognize those lies you've struggled with? Can you be honest with yourself, whether you've struggled for two days or twenty years? I hope you realize at this point that when you believe those lies, they can completely hijack your life.

But here's the good news.

Romans 8:5-6 tells us that this works both ways: "Those who live according to the flesh have their minds set on what the flesh desires; but those who live in accordance with the Spirit have their minds set on what the Spirit desires. The mind governed by the flesh is death, but the mind governed by the Spirit is life and peace."

In other words:

Living according to worldly beliefs and desires = Death
Living according to God's truths and desires = Life

So how do you take a mind programmed with worldly lies and reprogram it with godly desires?

That's right . . .

Consult Your Instruction Manual

It only makes sense that when you get a new mind—just like when you get anything else new—you'll go to your good ol' instruction manual.

A lot of times when you buy something new, there's one of those little stickers on the product or on the manual itself that says, "Read the instruction manual in its entirety before use." I highly recommend this practice with *your* instruction manual too. There's so much good stuff in the Bible. Between Noah and the Nativity, before and after John 3:16, there is action, mystery, and romance—no kidding! But most important, therein lies God's message just for you. He wrote you a big long letter. Read it.

INSTRUCTIONS:

1. Go to a bookstore, the library, your church, BibleGateway .com, or the YouVersion app. God has made sure there are endless Bible resources, just for you.

2. Read a few different versions and passages and choose the style that really speaks to you. Find a version you can understand. Find one that's comfortable, enjoyable, that you *like* to read. From the formal, literary language of the King James Version to the passionate message of, well, *The Message*, there's a version of the Bible that is your perfect instruction manual.

3. Select a method of delivery. Do you want a paper Bible to highlight, jot notes in, and flip through? Or do you want to read it on your laptop? Or take it with you on your phone and send Scriptures to everyone with a touch of a screen? What about an audio Bible that reads to you? It's now so very easy to have the entire Bible — every version, every language — in your pocket every single second of the day. There's no excuse for not reading the Bible; it's available pretty much any way you want it!

4. Choose a reading plan. There are a gazillion reading plans out there. You can buy Bibles with plans printed in the back or with the text already broken into daily readings in both paper and electronic copies. You can read the Scriptures chronologically, as it happened, or from Genesis to Revelation. Or Revelation to Genesis. You can read a chapter a day. You can read the whole thing in ninety days. You can read it in three years. As. Long. As. You. Read. It.

5. Start reading! And stick to it. There's something that happens in this process. First, of course, you're ingesting little pieces of God's Word. Every single day. But you're also developing a spiritually healthy habit. It's a daily commitment to your relationship with God. And when you stay with it, your relationship, your faith, only grows stronger.

I understand that it's a huge undertaking. (Remember? I'm the dumb kid who can't read.) But stick with it. You won't be sorry.

I can't do it for you. This book doesn't even come close. Your preacher, your mom, your teacher can't make you. Like everything else, it's a choice. (Unlike almost everything else, it's a *good* choice.)

You never know: There could be a little tiny verse, hidden right in the middle of some obscure passage, in one of those books that you can't pronounce — maybe Habakkuk — that says, "To find your superpowers, click your heels three times and say the magic words: . . ."

It could be there.

How will you ever know?

Right. You'll have to read it for yourself.

(And when you do, you *will* find super-power Scripture. I did.)

Faith Comes by Hearing

It may be a day, it may be a year, but I promise you, if you will commit to renewing your mind and staying in God's Word, walking daily in his truth, you will begin to know a faith that you never even knew existed. You'll not only be more strongly equipped to combat lies and temptations but you'll also become more in tune with God's will and purpose for your life. And when you walk in that purpose, trust me, your life is just a better place to be.

Whether you realize it or not, you are choosing, with each passing moment, what to use as the source that feeds your soul and spirit. If you're not hearing the Word of God, you're choosing something else to fill you up.

Life or Death? Up to You.

Proverbs 18:20-21 says,

> From the fruit of their mouth a person's stomach is filled;
>   with the harvest of their lips they are satisfied.
> The tongue has the power of life and death,
>   and those who love it will eat its fruit.

So the things that we take in, in this example, are like fruit, and you're going to be satisfied by what you speak from your lips. It also tells us that "the tongue has the power of life and death." Everything you speak today is either speaking life or speaking death, and whichever one you're thinking on and speaking is the one you're going to be satisfied by. Whether good or evil, you will be satisfied by those things.

I want you to take inventory of your thoughts. I want you to really think about the things you say about yourself or the things you think about. Maybe they're things that have been said about you. Maybe they're things that you tell yourself when you look in the mirror every day. But take a minute to consider the words you hear rolling around in your mind. Proverbs 6:2 warns, "You have been trapped by what you said, ensnared by the words of your mouth." Are your words speaking life? Are they positive, life-giving thoughts? Or are they speaking death? Destruction? Detriment? Your words have the power of life or death.

You've got to understand and see that what you give attention to will grow. For example, let's say you take two plants and you put them outside. One seed is good; the other seed is bad. You give more attention to one than the other. I don't mean like your crazy grandma who talks to her thirty-five potted plants. I don't mean a conversation. The kind of attention I'm talking about is maybe you give them water. If you give one attention by watering it and you don't give any to the other one, eventually the one without water will die. The one you've watered will live. Which seed do you water, the good seed or the bad seed? The thoughts we give attention to are the thoughts we choose to water. When we water them, something will begin to sprout and grow. Whether they are thoughts of life or thoughts of death, the thoughts that get attention will be the plant that grows and thrives in your life.

If you hear you're stupid, you're dumb, you are never going to amount to anything, you're unlovable, you're wasted space, you're addicted, dirty, used, you're a failure, too much for anyone to handle, drama, suicidal, depressed, anxious, bulimic, gay, anorexic, ugly — um, you get the picture — long enough, you start to believe it, don't you? Maybe you *already* believe that one of these lies is true for you. If you've been hearing it, focusing on it, watering it, it's going to take root in your life. Whatever you choose to focus on and give value to, you will become. What you give attention to will begin to grow.

Using another seed metaphor, let's say that you were outside with your friends and they planted an apple seed. For days you guys kept watering that seed. If it eventually sprouted an apple, you are not going to be mad at your friends and say, "Oh my goodness! I cannot believe that apple seed sprouted an apple!" Right? You understand that what you put in the ground is an apple seed. If you give it attention and you water it, eventually that seed will grow into itself.

For the same reason, we shouldn't be surprised that when we feed and foster negative things in our lives, negative, destructive things come to pass. That is exactly what you are doing with your harmful words. You are planting seeds, and if you give them attention long enough, you'll eventually sprout something that you never wanted to be there. The more you repeat these toxic seeds in your own mind and speak them out loud about yourself, the more you will become them.

Here's what I want you to do right now: I want you to get out a piece of paper and something you can write with, and I want you to draw a line right down the middle of that piece of paper. On one side of that piece of paper, write "LIFE," and on the other side of that piece of paper, write "DEATH." Now take inventory of what is going on in your mind. Under the appropriate heading, write down every thought you have about yourself. And here's what I want you to know: Anything that makes you feel anxious, depressed, out of control, cloudy, confused, trapped, defeated, fearful—all of these things are not from God. They are rooted in evil and are from the Enemy. Hang on to this list. In the next chapter, we're going to replace all of those deadly lies with the truth of God's Word.

Harmony Within

Do you remember the circles representing the body, soul, and spirit? Remember that the soul is made up of the mind, will, and emotions? Well, when the Holy Spirit enters into the mix, it can split your spirit away from your soul. Let's face it: The soul (with your jumbled mind, strong will, and topsy-turvy emotions) isn't always right. But your spirit—now that the Holy Spirit is living within you—knows the truth. And if the soul and spirit are debating the truth within you, it can leave you feeling pretty confused.

The great thing is that you can always fill your mind with the truth of God's Word, allowing your emotions to follow. The Word always clarifies. If you are living in confusion right now, it's not because God is confusing you; it's because you have not gone to the Word and found what God's truth says about you. When both your soul and spirit are grounded in truth, everyone gets along just peachy.

Hebrews 4:12 tells us, "The word of God is alive and active. Sharper than any double-edged sword, it penetrates even to dividing soul and spirit, joints and marrow; it judges the thoughts and attitudes of the heart."

Let me explain the verse like this: Take both of your hands and interlock them like a cute couple would. Think of your left hand as your soul and your right as your spirit. This verse is saying that sometimes even though the soul and the spirit are two different things—just like your left and right hands—they feel interlocked. But in those moments when we feel confusion set in, we can't tell what is coming from our

emotions (soul) and what is the truth (Holy Spirit). Your new spirit responds only to the truth, and the sword (God's Word) will split the two. Always choose to go with the spirit over the soul.

It's a Process

Now, if you're starting to feel overwhelmed, thinking you've got to read the whole Bible today so you can act like an angel tomorrow . . .

Don't.

Remember, it's like an instruction manual.

Do you read an instruction manual cover to cover, all in one sitting?

No.

Do you finish it, thinking, *Hmmm, that was a heart-warming story*, and place it on your bookshelf to collect dust?

Nooo . . .

It's an instruction manual.

If you're trying to fix something—even if you've read the thing all the way through already—you pick it up, look for the section on whatever you're trying to fix, and you read that section, right? And if you're like me, while you're reading that part, you have the thing you're trying to fix or program right in front of you. You read steps one and two and then you apply them. You read a couple more steps and do a couple more things. Then after a repeated process of reading and doing and reading and doing, you've got the thing programmed and working the way it's supposed to.

And then it'll break. Or the batteries will die. And you have to go back and reread that section again.

I've learned that you've got to treat the Bible that way too. You don't sit down the day you become a Christian and read the whole instruction manual on how to operate your new self. First of all, if you can read the whole Bible in a day, you're already way ahead of the rest of us! And seriously, reading the Bible, getting into the Word, hearing God's will and plan for your life—that takes time. It's a daily process. It's dedicating each and every day to following God and equipping yourself with the tools to do it. It's not a one-day, one-reading, one-sitting thing.

It's a lifetime process . . .

Of trying . . .

Messing up . . .

Learning . . .

Falling down . . .

Getting back up . . .

And most important . . .

Trying again.

Tell the Truth

1. What are your favorite stories and passages in the Bible? What about them makes them memorable for you? What truths are they communicating?

2. Have you ever read the Bible all the way through? If you have, it never hurts to read it again. Take the next few minutes to research different Bible reading plans and choose one. (You might want to start by doing a search online or going to YouVersion.com.)

3. Have you found a Bible version you like? If not, close this book and find one now.

Truth Trumps Temptation

I BELIEVE THAT a lot of times the reason we continue to go through the cycles of sin is because of deception. Deception is a lie that hasn't yet been discovered. If someone understands and sees deception for what it is, it is not deception anymore; it becomes a lie. And I think it's only when we get to a place where we know the truth and are beginning to allow it to function in our lives that we can be free from the lies.

The Sneaky Serpent

One of the most effective methods the Enemy uses in deceiving us is getting to us when we are weak, often when we are alone. He is very well aware of our human weaknesses, and he knows how easy it is for us to be swayed into believing something when there isn't an outside party supporting us, evaluating the truth of what we're being told. And for both of these reasons, he loves to catch us when we're off all by ourselves, and he tells us that we're all alone in our messes. Go back and reread the story of Adam and Eve (see Genesis 3:1-13). I know, we've already talked about this a little in previous chapters, but I promise, we're digging a little deeper now.

When the Enemy brought his mess of doubt and pride into God's perfect garden, did you notice that he didn't approach Adam and Eve while they were in the presence of God? (God comes looking for them in verses 8-9.) He also didn't start with the big ol' strapping male. I'm guessing he selected the one more in touch with her feelings and started working on her emotions.

When the serpent told Eve that eating the fruit would make her like God, she probably felt betrayed, believing that God forbid them from eating the fruit only because he wanted to have an advantage over them. She might have begun to believe that God was being selfish. (I don't know about you, but it rubs me the wrong way when I feel as though someone is being selfish and unfair.) Not only that, but God told them that eating the fruit would mean death. The seeds of doubt the serpent planted about God's reasons for the command probably impacted her belief about his promised consequence of death as well. As these thoughts and feelings swirled around in her mind, the fruit began to appear harmless and desirable to Eve. We get hints to this in Genesis 3:6. Eve "saw" (sight) that the fruit "was good for food" (taste, craving) "and pleasing to the eye" (more than just sight—emotion-stirring beauty) "and also desirable for gaining wisdom" (appealing to the intellect).

I think it's safe to assume that Satan was intent on appealing to Eve's feelings and emotions. He preyed on her weakness, knowing that her pride could be elevated as she began to doubt whether or not God truly had her best interests at heart.

You may have found yourself in a similar
situation, being tempted to believe thoughts of
doubt and feelings of pride from the Enemy.
Aw, now, don't feel bad. He's not picking on you
in particular. I believe he's tried it on every single person on this
planet. He even tried it on the Son of God himself.

I mean, look at how Satan tried to tempt Jesus. He didn't
do it in front of a big crowd or while Jesus was surrounded by
his twelve disciples so that they could back him up; he waited
till Jesus was alone and tired and worn out. That's when he
came to him and tempted him (see Matthew 4:1-11).

What that sneaky serpent didn't know is this: Where Eve
and Adam were unprepared, Jesus was armed with the truth.

Truth Bombs from Jesus

Let's go way back, deep into the wilderness. Imagine that you're
on day forty of a forty-day fast. You might be a bit hungry, a
little weak, a tad desperate. (Understatement of the year, right?)

This is exactly where Jesus was. Alone. In the desert.
Hungry. Tired. Sure, he was the living Son of God, but he was
also human, just like us. Hebrews 4:15 explains, "We do not
have a high priest who is unable to empathize with our weaknesses, but we have one who has been tempted in every way,
just as we are—yet he did not sin."

So what did Jesus do differently from Adam and Eve, from
us? What was the top-secret tactic that allowed Jesus to walk
away before a mess was made?

Truth bombs.

That's right. Jesus had 'em, and he wasn't afraid to use 'em.

Check it out: "Then Jesus was led by the Spirit into the wilderness to be tempted by the devil. After fasting forty days and forty nights, he was hungry" (Matthew 4:1-2). That always makes me laugh. "He was hungry." Ketric Version of the Bible: "Dude, he was *starving*!" And notice where he was led? That's right: "into the wilderness," where Satan could have him all to himself.

"The tempter came to him and said, 'If you are the Son of God, tell these stones to become bread'" (verse 3). Now, Satan could've requested any miracle here to prove that Jesus was the Son of God. Why do you think he chose "bread"?

"Hey, Jesus, you know what sounds good right now? Yeah, some fresh-from-the-oven, piping-hot cinnamon rolls, oozing with creamy icing. Mmmm. Oh, wait. You're the Son of God. You could just speak and they'd appear, right? Well, what are you waiting for, man? Let's eat!" (Ketric Version).

And starving, in the wilderness, how did Jesus reply? "It is written: 'Man shall not live on bread alone, but on every word that comes from the mouth of God'" (verse 4).

Ka-BLAOW!

And that's the power of the Word of God. When you don't have the willpower within your human body to defeat evil, the Word of God (if you're equipped with it) will be the power that you lack. It's the weapon Eve and Adam didn't understand they had access to.

Satan was thrown for a loop at Jesus' response. *Okay, this isn't going to be as easy as I thought. He hasn't eaten in forty days, and still, food didn't get him. But I bet power will.* And then, the Devil double-dog-dares the Son of God.

"Oh yeah, well, then throw yourself off the temple if you're so high and mighty" (Ketric Version). But then Satan does something *really* interesting: He quotes the Bible back to Jesus. (I'm imagining a mocking, first-grader tone here.) Satan tells him, "It is written: 'He will command his angels concerning you, and they will lift you up in their hands, so that you will not strike your foot against a stone'" (verse 6).

It's worth noting here that Satan took the very source that Jesus trusted and believed in and turned it around, manipulated the meaning, and tried to use it as a tool for temptation. Sound familiar? Believe me, he's gonna try this on you, too. And when he does, we already have the solution. Watch what Jesus does.

"It is also written: 'Do not put the Lord your God to the test'" (verse 7).

BAM! Truth bomb number two!

But Satan doesn't know when to give up.

Greed. Oh yeah, greed gets 'em all. Hey, demons, watch this!

"Again, the devil took him to a very high mountain and showed him all the kingdoms of the world and their splendor. 'All this I will give you,' he said, 'if you will bow down and worship me'" (verses 8-9).

I can almost hear Jesus snickering here. I mean, really? Satan is going to give kingdoms to the Creator of the universe? Riiight.

Jesus has now had enough. "Away from me, Satan! For it is written: 'Worship the Lord your God, and serve him only.'

Then the devil left him, and angels came and attended him" (verses 10-11).

Temptation Versus Truth

Jesus had this thing down. With all three of Satan's temptations, Jesus used the same tactic: He truth-bombed Satan's lies every single time. And it worked.

Temptation Versus Truth (Matthew 4)	
IF YOU ARE THE SON OF GOD, TELL THESE STONES TO BECOME BREAD. (VERSE 3)	IT IS WRITTEN: "MAN SHALL NOT LIVE ON BREAD ALONE, BUT ON EVERY WORD THAT COMES FROM THE MOUTH OF GOD." (VERSE 4)
IF YOU ARE THE SON OF GOD . . . THROW YOURSELF DOWN. (VERSE 6)	IT IS ALSO WRITTEN: "DO NOT PUT THE LORD YOUR GOD TO THE TEST." (VERSE 7)
ALL THIS I WILL GIVE YOU . . . IF YOU WILL BOW DOWN AND WORSHIP ME. (VERSE 9)	AWAY FROM ME, SATAN! FOR IT IS WRITTEN: "WORSHIP THE LORD YOUR GOD, AND SERVE HIM ONLY." (VERSE 10)

Did you notice how easily Satan gave up here? And think about it: Jesus was the biggest prize in the history of the universe! Imagine the party that would break out in the underworld if only Satan could successfully tempt the one and only

Son of God. Those minions would be raving! But after a few tries, Satan just sort of slunk away. Sure, he came back for more, but Jesus—out in the wilderness, weak and tired and hungry—made Satan a little less confident in his skill of manipulation. Jesus defeated that serpent with the power of the truth.

And we can too.

Imagine if Eve had hung in there, if she had tossed a few truth bombs in that ol' serpent's face and if her garden companion had backed her up with truth bombs too.

Imagine if we had.

Well, imagine no longer.

Let's throw some truth bombs at our messes today. Take out that "LIFE/DEATH" sheet we worked on in the previous chapter. We're going to leave the LIFE things alone. Those are already good; keep them right where they are. But the DEATH you're speaking into your life—well, we're gonna get rid of it right now.

Make another chart similar to the "LIFE/DEATH" one. Write "TEMPTATION" on the left and "TRUTH" on the right. List the DEATH items you had written before under the "TEMPTATION" header. Now—this is so important—I want you to look in your Bible and find Scriptures that say the opposite of what's on that list. Write those truths in the TRUTH column and cross out that lie, that death-speaking temptation.

Spend as much time as you need here. Just do one or two at a time, if you need to, *but do it*! If you get hung up on one, use a Bible concordance or search for the general category on a Bible site or app. Or ask a pastor or parent. Just get it done. Seriously.

Here are a few references to help you out:

1. ~~I'm worthless.~~ See Psalm 139:14.
2. ~~I have no future.~~ See Jeremiah 29:11.
3. ~~My parents are idiots.~~ See Exodus 20:12.
4. ~~No one even knows I exist.~~ See 1 Corinthians 8:3.
5. ~~This exercise won't work.~~ See 2 Timothy 3:17.

Until you can replace the lies in your life with the truth, you will continue to focus on those lies and allow them to rule your life, forcing you to fall back into the same patterns and temptations over and over again. When you begin to focus on God's truth, you will experience that freedom found only through a walk with God.

For me, I believed I was addicted to pornography so much that it just became the norm for me. I allowed it to overtake my mind, and I gave in. But that all changed when I began to replace that lie with God's truth. At first I wasn't truly walking in freedom, but I continued to speak what God said about me instead of what my actions showed about me. Eventually, as I relentlessly spoke God's truth, I began to walk in freedom.

Rally the Troops

And here's the crazy thing about Satan: He doesn't have any new tricks. He's not making new ones up every day. Satan has only so many tricks up his sleeve, and he will use the same ones over and over for each and every one of us. By sticking together, we can recognize his tricks and tactics and be stronger in fighting against them. When you and I get to the place where we don't want to be alone anymore and we begin to share what's happened in our lives and the thoughts going through our heads, we will be amazed at how many other people around us are actually dealing with the same things. Satan's using those same old crazy schemes on everyone. There's nothing new under the sun. You and I are a product of Adam and Eve, people who, when finding themselves in issues and struggles and messes, hid themselves. They didn't run *to* help but ran *away* from help.

I find myself doing this very same thing, and it blows me away. Instead of running to people around me for truth and love, I run from them. Have you ever considered that Jesus had twelve people around him? If the Son of God surrounded himself with twelve people, why is it that you and I don't think we need people around us to comfort us, love on us, and pray for us? Our own Savior did! If Jesus Christ had someone around him, supporting him all the time, you and I should too.

Know Your Ammo

Remember, it's a spiritual war out there. But you and I have been given the spiritual knowledge, authority, and power to win each battle. Go back and look at the armor of God mentioned in chapter 5. Study God's Word in order to stock up on those truth bombs. Surround yourself with other troops in the army of truth. Rely on them to have your back, and when they're in trouble, be sure to loan them a truth bomb or two.

I know it's not easy. If it were, it'd be called recess instead of spiritual warfare. But if we equip ourselves with God's Word, practice using it, and stick together in truth, we can become skilled and effective fighters in the battle for our souls.

Tell the Truth

1. Are you finished with your Truth Versus Temptation chart?

2. Hey, you know that chart we talked about? Did you complete it?

3. I've got an idea. Why don't you work on your Truth Versus Temptation chart?

4. Do I sound just like your mom? (It's because I care. Just like she does.) Take the time today or over the next week or so to complete the chart. You might be surprised at some of the truths you find in God's Word.

The Truth Lives in You

WHEN I GAVE my life to Jesus, someone handed me *The Message* Bible, and for the first time in my entire life, a book made sense. It was crazy! I would pick up that Bible, and all of its words and sentences and pages—which should have been overwhelming to a learning-disabled kid like me—made perfect sense. I was so pumped that I would tell *everyone* about what I was reading and how it was changing my life. I remember going to Bible studies and telling people, "Oh my gosh, you *have* to read this book! The stories are phenomenal!" And I'd tell them a story or two and they would stand up and clap for me. For me!

I remember the summer before eighth grade. I was reading my Bible and these words popped out in 2 Corinthians 12:9: "My grace is sufficient for you, for my power is made perfect in weakness." At that very moment, God took a lie that I had believed ever since first grade—that I was dumb and that I was never going to be used by God—and he began to speak his truth into that lie. I knew that God was saying something to me that day, and it was this: "Ketric, I'm going to take the

99

thing that you think has no power, that could never be used by me, that thing you're ashamed of, and I will use it for my glory. When I do, you will not be able to take the credit. People will know it is not you but *me in you* that they see."

Pretty profound for an eighth grader, huh? But it was true then, and it's still true today. All through elementary school, I was in a learning-disability class. I felt dumb, useless. But now—through the truth, power, and glory of God—guess what? That disability doesn't hinder me. In fact, I'm now an *author*. Weird.

Expect the Unexpected

When I was a sophomore in high school, we moved to this town called Enid, Oklahoma. Probably within the first month of living there, I met these guys. They were the first guys I had really started making any connection with, so one night at about eleven thirty, I decided it would be a good idea for all of those guys to stay at my house.

Let me set the house up for you. When you walked through the front doors, if you can visualize this, to the right there was a couch. At the end of the couch there was a lamp. To the left was my parents' bedroom. So when we got to the door, I told my buddy James to go ahead and walk in my living room, head off to the back of the house, and be quiet going back to my room.

Now close your eyes for just a second or two.

Go on, do it.

There. That's how dark it was in my house that night.

So James heads into the house, but as he's walking, he—*thud*—runs into the couch. Stumbling around, he finds his way around the couch, but he—*crash!*—knocks over the lamp. No, actually, it was more like, *CRASH!!!* I'm not joking; it was one of the loudest noises I've ever heard. I looked to my left, and my eyes at that moment had started to adjust to the darkness of the room. To my surprise, I'm making out a picture of a silhouette of what looks to be my dad. As my eyes focus more, I realize that my dad is standing there in the living room.

In his underwear.

Now, my father is one of the cutest things you've ever seen. I know I told you he's a Little Debbie man and even fits that role perfectly. He's so cute! I'm not kidding. Some of you on the weekend, you go to churches that have you greet each other. They tell you to shake hands, and then they say, "Tell someone around you hello." If I were in church with you and my dad was standing next to me and they told you to greet someone around you, he's so cute you would want to pick him up and just cuddle him. You might just want to take him and put him in your pocket—he's that cute. All five foot three of him, with his soft voice, bald head, and mustache.

However, my father is also a very frugal man. He's always been good with his money. When he buys clothes, he wears them until they fall apart. And that goes for his undies, too. He'll wear those babies until they're completely worn out, all stretched out with holes in the rear. The tighty whities weren't so white-y anymore, if you know what I'm sayin'. Maybe he's trying to go green, with his own crazy version of reduce, reuse, and recycle. Not cool, Dad. I don't think it's cool. And I'm pretty sure *cool* was not the first word on my friends' minds either.

But I digress.

So as my eyes continued to adjust to the room, I began to realize that my dad was hunkered down in a squatting position in his underwear, with both fists in the air, and there was a weird noise coming out of his mouth. As I listened closer, I realized that those were words that were coming out of my father's mouth. Like a bawking chicken, he was clucking, "What, what, what, what, what!"

Right there in that moment, I really didn't know what to do. I couldn't tell if he was messing with me and just playing around or if he was seriously doing the chicken dance in his underwear. Did he think someone was breaking into our house? And this is his defense? I don't know about you, but if I broke into someone's house and I had a five-foot bald-headed man in his underwear bawking, "What, what, what, what, what, what!" I'm pretty sure I'm putting down the flat-screen TV and hightailing it out of there!

Not knowing how to react, I decided to grab his arms. I said to him, "Dad, it's me! Go back to bed!"

But my dad didn't respond.

Well, I guess he sort of did.

He kept saying, "What, what, what, what!"

So I got up super close to my dad and focused in really hard on his face. I looked at him straight in his mustache, and that's when I realized that my father was completely asleep. That's right, I said asleep. My father was standing in the living room, saying, "What, what, what, what," and he was completely asleep. He had no clue what was going on.

Then, to top it off, my mom emerges. In her night-
gown. So all of a sudden, these new guys that I just
had met are getting to meet my family in the best
possible way. But my mom finally does get my
dad to go to bed, and the next morning when
we talk about the situation, he remembers nothing. That's all
fine and dandy for him, but that image is ingrained in my
brain forever!

So why in the world am I telling you this? Well, for one, it's
part of my therapy. But, seriously, my point is this: Expect the
unexpected.

One might say that my dad, the bawking chicken, bears
some similarities to that biblical burning bush. How, you
ask? Well, for one, that image was probably burned in Moses'
mind forever. And, two, it was completely, utterly, absolutely
unexpected.

Let's take a look.

In Exodus, chapter 3, Moses was going about his normal
day. He wasn't expecting anything different. He was a shepherd at the time. He spent his days with a flock of sheep, caring
for them and looking after them.

But Exodus 3 tells us about the bawking chicken that enters
Moses' life:

> Moses was tending the flock of Jethro his father-in-law, the
> priest of Midian, and he led the flock to the far side of the
> wilderness and came to Horeb, the mountain of God. There
> the angel of the LORD appeared to him in flames of fire from
> within a bush. Moses saw that though the bush was on fire
> it did not burn up. So Moses thought, "I will go over and see

this strange sight—why the bush does not burn up."

When the Lord saw that he had gone over to look, God called to him from within the bush, "Moses! Moses!"

And Moses said, "Here I am."

"Do not come any closer," God said. "Take off your sandals, for the place where you are standing is holy ground." Then he said, "I am the God of your father, the God of Abraham, the God of Isaac and the God of Jacob." At this, Moses hid his face, because he was afraid to look at God. (verses 1-6)

Much like my own story, Moses is just going about his normal day, when the unexpected happens. He sees a bush that's on fire, and then it starts talking to him! He wasn't expecting anything new to happen; he was just expecting to go and do his job. But God interrupted his schedule that day and took him on a journey. God told him that he was going to be the one to take the Israelites from Egypt—from Pharaoh's hands—to the Promised Land.

Moses' Buts

Let's pause and cover a little background of Moses' life prior to this unexpected event. Moses was born into an Israelite family. At the time, the Egyptians were using the Israelites as forced labor and actively sought to kill the newborn male children in order to keep the Israelites from becoming too powerful. In a miraculous sequence of events, Moses was not killed at birth; instead, he grew up in the household of Pharaoh, escaping the fate of being a slave to the Egyptians like the rest of his people were. He later fled Egypt after killing an Egyptian who was abusing an Israelite and then settled in Midian, where he became a shepherd. (Now we are caught up to the event of the bush.)

So when Moses learned over the course of his conversation with God that God expected him to return to Egypt and lead the Israelites out of the land, Moses immediately put on the brakes. "Who am I that I should go to Pharaoh and bring the Israelites out of Egypt?" (Exodus 3:11). Remember, when Moses left Egypt, he was wanted for murder. What would await him if he returned?

And God replies, "I will be with you" (verse 12).

Shouldn't that be enough? Shouldn't that be all that Moses—or any of us—needs to hear? There's a bush. It's on fire. But the leaves are not burning. And it's talking to you. Telling you that God himself is speaking. Giving you directions. And saying, "I will be with you." Do we really need to know anything else?

Moses is talking to a bush, yet he's the one questioning God?

And Moses doesn't stop there. He continues to doubt and question and give hypotheticals.

"But, but, God . . . what if they don't believe me? What if I go and I tell people what God has told me, and all of a sudden the people around me don't believe me?" (Ketric Version).

Isn't that how the Enemy works? He creates doubt. He invites us to dwell on the super-long list of what-ifs. But here's a what-if for ya: What if we just trusted God?

If we're dwelling on the worry and doubt that Satan is presenting, with all of his bells and whistles, does that mean we're choosing to trust Satan's word over God's?

This is serious, people.

We have something that God has spoken to us, and we're supposed to believe that Word by faith, even though we don't see any physical signs yet. Hebrews 11:1 reminds us of this: "Faith is confidence in what we hope for and assurance about what we do not see."

If God is about *faith*, the Enemy is most definitely about *doubt*. Satan is constantly trying to get us to doubt what God has said, what God has told us about our lives. And that is what is happening to Moses here. And I think all of us have asked, *God, what if what I heard was wrong and what you said I was supposed to do, my talents and my abilities and my purpose, are all wrong? What if I read this book, and I get some truth, and I believe it to be true, and I believe that faith does come by hearing, and I begin to start changing my life in getting free from addictions and hurts and ex-girlfriends and stuff, and I tell the world that I've changed, and what if they laugh at me, and what if I let them down, and what if, what if, what if?!*

(My editor's gonna love that last sentence.)

It's all fear.

So many of the troubles you and I face on a daily basis are built on fear. And if you look back at the things you've feared over the past couple years, you'll probably realize that the things you feared aren't even issues anymore. Second Timothy 1:7 says, "God has not given us a spirit of fear, but of power and of love and of a sound mind" (NKJV). So if you feel fear, it is not from God. God is not passing out fear.

Now, there is a healthy fear and there is an unhealthy fear. Fearing God can be a healthy fear. But fearing a circumstance, especially when it causes you to doubt God as a result, is not a healthy fear. If something gives you anxiety, depression, or confusion, it is not from God. Read that verse again. He did not give you a spirit of fear but a spirit of power, love, and a sound mind. If you don't feel as though you have a sound mind right now, you can. He has already given it to you.

Did you know that more than 360 times in the Bible God had to tell his people not to fear or be afraid? I believe that is because that is one of the biggest ways the Enemy will get you to stop moving forward toward what God has for you and living in freedom.

Over the last year or so, God has been saying to me, "Ketric, if Satan can't get you to deny it, he will get you to delay it." Isn't that so true? If Satan can't get you to deny what God wants to do in and through your life, he will get you to delay it with *whens*, *thens*, and *if onlys*. Satan wants all of us to sit in the delayed state of saying, "Well, it's not that I don't believe it; I just need to wait on the timing."

And I totally get that. Sometimes God does want us to wait on his timing, but there comes a moment when we've already prayed about it. We already know what God wants us to do and we're just not willing to step into it because of fear.

I remember when I was on staff at Lifechurch.tv and my pastor, Craig, told a story one time that changed my world. He started talking about a scarecrow and began asking the audience what does the scarecrow do? Does it move around? Does it jump off the stake it's on and begin to run around and scare the crows away from the crop? No! It doesn't do anything. The only thing the scarecrow does is sit there. It doesn't move. It doesn't talk. Its only job is to put fear in the crows so they won't come toward the good crop. If crows were smart, they would just go past the scarecrow because on the other side of the scarecrow is where the best crop lives.

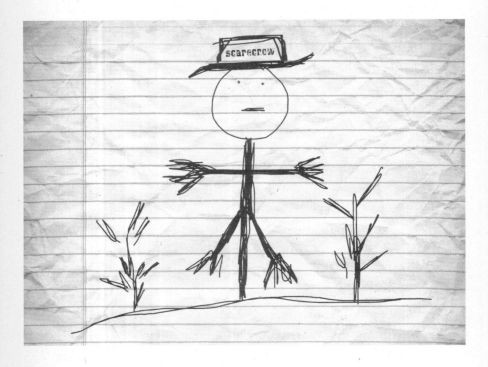

The same thing is true for you and me. That scarecrow is our fears. Those fears can't do anything to us. They can't move. They can't grab us. They can only scare us and try to get us to delay what is already ours and keep us away from the good crop: what God has for us. You and I need to bust through the fear. We need to tackle those dumb scarecrows and feast on the best crops, where our purposes and lives are.

Let the Truth Shine Through

Continuing on in the story about Moses' life, we find Moses still making excuses. In Exodus 4:10, Moses reminded God, his Creator, "I have never been eloquent, neither in the past nor since you have spoken to your servant. I am slow of speech and tongue."

(And I'll just note here that Moses didn't seem too slow of speech *or* tongue when he was trying to tell God how incapable he was.)

I love God's response here: "Who gave human beings their mouths? . . . Is it not I, the LORD?" (verse 11). God just gave it to Moses straight. "Moses I don't need to hear your opinion about yourself. I don't need you to tell me what *you* think you were made to do on this earth. You didn't make you; I made you. And I know what you are made to do" (Ketric Version). The best thing for Moses to do was just shut his mouth and let God shine through.

Don't Put God in a Box

And before we get too judgmental of Moses, we need to think about our own *buts*, our own excuses, our own arguments with God.

"God, I'm just not smart enough."

"I'm addicted."

"I can't."

"I don't have time."

"I don't want to be prideful."

Christians use that last one a lot. But you see, pride can be two different things: Pride can be boasting or talking yourself up about something you're not, or pride can be talking yourself down when God says something that you are. Yep, that's also pride. But we don't see it that way. When we tell ourselves and the world around us that we're nothing special, that we're just trying to get by, that we're just trying to survive, that's not humility at all. What you are actually doing is denying God to work in your life and through your life and not allowing him to do the big things he wants to do.

The story of Moses represents this struggle so well. Moses would deny and question his abilities, and God would lift him up and prove him wrong. Miracle after miracle, Moses still didn't get it. Through all of the burning bushes, staffs morphing into snakes, water turning to blood, Moses continued to question and doubt. I mean, if God did those crazy signs for us, we would trust him with the rest of the journey, wouldn't we?

Or would we?

We compartmentalize so many things in our lives. It's like we say to God, "Okay, God, here's the deal. I'll give a relationship. Like, I'll give you my heart and all that. But when it comes to some of these other things in my life, don't worry about all that. I will take care of it. It's my problem, and I can figure it out myself." It's crazy, isn't it? But we all do this as human beings. We see God doing a work in our lives, and we trust him with some parts of our lives, but we don't trust him with it completely.

We think it's okay to compartmentalize God, to put him in a box. It's an iPod playlist. You know what I mean. People don't buy CDs as much as they used to. The majority will buy one song off this CD, or one song off that CD, and buy whatever songs they feel like. We take the songs we like and leave the songs out that we don't like, and we call it our playlist.

I believe we also do this with God. We don't buy the whole God CD. We choose the parts of God that we want and drag them over into our God playlist. "Oh yeah, God, I'll give you my summer camp or my Wednesday nights. Sundays, too. I'll give you my sin. I'll give you my life. Well, sorta. When it comes to the girl you want me to date, I got that. I mean, you don't know anything about dating anyway, God. I know about dating, so I'll take it from here."

But God doesn't work that way. You see, God wants to be a part of every journey we go on — every part of our lives.

And that is what he was trying to get Moses to see.

How Big Is Your God?

Only through the grace and power of God, Moses finally gets those Israelites away from Pharaoh. He's standing at the edge of the Red Sea, probably feeling pretty powerful, the hero of the Israelites, when he hears a noise — a very, very bad noise. It's the sound of horses galloping and soldiers yelling and chariots thundering.

"Um, God? It's me, Moses. You can help me now."

Now, the first time I read God's response in the Bible, I really didn't understand it.

"Then the LORD said to Moses, 'Why are you crying out to me? Tell the Israelites to move on'" (Exodus 14:15).

"Um, ahem, God, can you repeat that? It sorta sounded like you told me to . . . to move on?" (Ketric Version).

Why would God say this? Doesn't he know that Moses is standing before the Red Sea with God's children, the Israelites, and there are six hundred chariots coming from behind to kill them all? Doesn't he get it? Doesn't he understand that the Promised Land is on the other side of the Red Sea?

I believe that God is saying, "I know, you big dummy!" Okay, God wouldn't call us dummies, but I think God is telling Moses, "I already know your situation, Moses. Stop telling me about your Red Sea, and start telling your Red Sea about *me*."

Did you get that?

And I believe that the same words that he spoke to Moses are the same words he's speaking to you and me. He's saying to us, "Stop telling me about your addiction, cutting, alcoholism, drug addiction, bulimia, anorexia, depression, and anxiety, and start telling them about *me*."

We all have things in our lives that we think are bigger than God. I know we don't say that out loud, we may not even think it, but we certainly act like it. We act like we don't trust God to take over the Red Seas in our lives.

One of my Red Seas was definitely pornography. I was so focused on pornography that it became bigger than the God I served. And that is an absolute lie from hell. God has given us the ability to overcome everything the Enemy throws at us because the Spirit of God is placed inside us. We just have to embrace it, trust it, and let it shine through.

My pastor used to say, "You are not fighting *for* victory but *from* victory." You have already been given everything you need to fight what is before you, but sometimes there are certain things you and I must do in the natural to make the supernatural happen.

At the Red Sea, the second part of God's reply is this: "Raise your staff and stretch out your hand over the sea to divide the water so that the Israelites can go through the sea on dry ground" (Exodus 14:16). This is a great reminder that sometimes there are things we must do in the natural to make the supernatural happen. Moses had to step into the water and stretch out his hand and put his staff in the water. When he did that, the water parted and Moses and the Israelites walked through on dry land.

Sometimes, many times, God is just asking us to step out in faith.

We Are Weak, but He Is Strong

You sang "Jesus Loves Me" as a kid, didn't you? If you're like me, you just stood there, sorta rolling out the words, not really thinking about or knowing what they meant. But now that I'm older, I get it: "They are weak, but he is strong."

If God can work through Moses and he can work through me, he can shine through you, too. That's exactly what Paul is talking about in 2 Corinthians 12. He realized that through his weakness, God's power is made perfect. God's glory can shine through even more brightly. Paul goes on to say, "Therefore I will boast all the more gladly about my weaknesses, so that Christ's power may rest on me" (verse 9).

So whatever your weaknesses may be, don't be ashamed of them. Don't hide them. Lift them up to God and say, "Here, God. See if you can do something with *these*."

You're a complete and total loser?

Good.

The more weaknesses you have, the more God's power will shine through you.

We're Only the Package

Back in the day, I worked my dad's Little Debbie route. He would sell Oatmeal Creme Pies, Zebra Cakes, Swiss Rolls, Nutty Bars. Man, I love the Zebra Cakes. I could lick the stripes off a Zebra Cake quicker than anybody else.

One day when I was working my dad's route, I was walking into this gas station with a twenty-four-pack of Oatmeal Creme Pies. And I promise you, I'm not crazy, but God spoke to me through an Oatmeal Creme Pie. I felt as if God said, "Ketric, you're just the package." At that moment, I didn't know what it meant.

But I began to realize what he was saying. When people want to buy an Oatmeal Creme Pie, they are not going in there to buy the package; they're paying their money for what is *in* the package. In the same way, your worth, your strength, your power isn't your body, your outside. It's Christ—the way, the truth, and the light—living inside of you. It is Christ in you that is going to resist the lie, live out God's purpose, live the Christian life. It was that day that I finally realized I could be free from pornography. God wasn't asking me to fix my problem; he was just asking me to surrender my superficial self so the good stuff inside would shine through. What is the superficial packaging in your life that you need to surrender?

Tell the Truth

1. Has God ever shown up in unexpected ways in your life? How did you respond?

2. Do you have a God playlist, or are you allowing God to work through every area of your life?

3. What Red Seas are you facing today? Why don't you go tell them how big your God is?

The Truth Will Set You Free

A FEW YEARS back, my sister-in-law's brother did something we could not fathom. One summer, after he had just gone through a divorce, he walked into his ex-wife's house, pulled out a gun, and shot and killed her. Then he turned the gun on himself.

We were blindsided.

We were all walking around asking the same question: Why in the world would God allow this to happen?

The crazy thing is that he was keeping a journal about what was going on in his life. About five days before he killed her and killed himself, he wrote something in his journal that disturbs me to this day. He wrote, "I'm lying here on my floor, and there is something after me. God help me, God help me, God help me!"

When I read that, it made me so mad. I didn't understand why in the world God didn't help him. And I wasn't the only one. It only compounded people's anger and confusion when, at the funeral, loved ones told wonderful stories of how caring this man was and how he had spoken to them about God. He was a believer who witnessed to others and spoke of putting Christ first in their lives.

How could someone like this ever contemplate such a thing?

This type of event will shake people's faith to the core. It will give them nightmares for months. This brand of evil is supposed to happen to someone else; it certainly isn't the type of thing that happens to good Christian men. Is it?

After the fog cleared and the numbness subsided, a few things came into focus. This type of tragedy doesn't just happen overnight; it starts with a small lie and grows into others. "You are a failure as a husband." "You are going to lose 'thing." "You are a bad father for not keeping the family together." "You are in too deep." "You will never be able to fix all the problems you created." "You have no other way out."

If we speak and think these lies enough, we start to believe them and they manifest into real problems in our lives. Then comes the mistake of asking God to just fix it, to put it back the way it used to be. *Please, God, turn back the clock and let me have a do-over.* We don't resist evil anymore because evil has weakened our will to resist. God has been helping and continues to help us, but we become so confused and caught in the fog of lies and despair that we can't see God's light to lead us back to safety.

If I had never known it before, I certainly learned it through this tragedy: Spiritual warfare is truly a life-or-death situation. Two people died that day because of the shackles of evil, making me only more determined in my mission of sharing the freedom that God's truth will bring.

Know this, my friends: When you are in Christ, you are completely, totally, absolutely free from the bonds of evil. You have power and authority over the dark forces at work in the world. You have everything you need inside of you to win the battle for your soul. And when you work toward God's purpose for your life, you will help and protect those fighting the battle alongside you.

Is Jesus Just a Ticket to Heaven?

In seventh grade, during spring break, the second time I ever stepped foot in a church, I gave my life to Jesus. No one told me to. No one had given me a Bible. I just knew it was what I was supposed to do. Have you ever felt that way?

I never had a second thought about it. I never wondered if I was saved. I never looked back and thought, *Man, maybe I need to give my life to Christ again.* I knew from the moment I gave my life to Jesus that he changed me. I knew there would come a day when Jesus would come back, or I would pass away, and I would go to heaven. Really, that was the extent of my relationship with Jesus.

I think there's a big piece of Jesus that we have left out. The church talks so much about how you need him to save you so you can get to heaven. But I believe that the church has done Christian believers—and unbelievers alike—a disservice by not fervently teaching about the battle that is going on in our lives, as well as the role Jesus plays in that battle. You know, I do think I heard verses quoted or the subject touched on sometime in church, but no one helped me fully understand what I really had through Jesus and what I would face in my Christian walk.

Now, I'm not downplaying the fact that Jesus Christ covered us with his blood and how significant and amazing that is. But what I want you to know is that Jesus Christ is even *more* than all that. Jesus took our sins on the cross and also all of God's wrath so you and I could walk free. Not only do we have a ticket to heaven but we also have been given the power over anything that comes into our lives. It is our job to use that power, that authority, against Satan and everything demonic that tries to kill, steal, and destroy.

In Romans 7, Paul spoke about something I've heard in church for a long time: "We know that the law is spiritual; but I am unspiritual, sold as a slave to sin. I do not understand what I do. For what I want to do I do not do, but what I hate I do. And if I do what I do not want to do, I agree that the law is good" (verses 14-16). When I heard that verse growing up, I always thought, *Okay, if Paul can't even control himself, then how in the world am I ever going to be able to control myself?*

Then as you go and read verse 17, Paul said, "As it is, it is no longer I myself who do it, but it is sin living in me." That one I really didn't get. What does it mean that it's not Paul who sins? Isn't he the one who is sinning? Then it clicked: He was refusing to associate himself with sin anymore. He realizes that he is now complete because the Spirit resides in him.

He is not his past, what he's done, or what he does; he is what Christ did.

You see, Paul realized from the moment he gave his life to Christ that there were still things in his soul that needed to be renewed. Like we talked about in chapter 8, it's a process. But you have to wrap your mind around the thought that you are not what you used to be or even what you are now.

In Romans 6:16-18, Paul wrote,

> Don't you know that when you offer yourselves to someone as obedient slaves, you are slaves of the one you obey — whether you are slaves to sin, which leads to death, or to obedience, which leads to righteousness? But thanks be to God that, though you used to be slaves to sin, you have come to obey from your heart the pattern of teaching that has now claimed your allegiance. You have been set free from sin and have become slaves to righteousness.

In this verse, when he said that you used to be slaves to sin, note that he was speaking in past tense. It's what you *used to be*, not what you are anymore. You once had a ball and chain around your ankle that was sin. When Jesus Christ died on the cross, he took off that ball and chain of sin and it became a ball and chain of righteousness. You don't have the key; nothing you could ever do is going to take that ball and chain off your leg. What's ironic, though, is that ball and chain is *freedom*. You are righteous because of what God has said about you. That is who you are, and that is the message God has been trying to get to his people for more than two thousand years.

Paul did his best to help God get the word out. He tried to tell us over and over that we are new creatures in Christ. In

Colossians 3:3, he said, "You died, and your life is now hidden with Christ in God." In Galatians 2:20, he wrote, "I have been crucified with Christ and I no longer live, but Christ lives in me." What Paul wanted to get into our brains is that the moment we give our lives to Christ, our old life dies.

You see, you are not a sinner anymore.

You've been freed.

If you still think you're a sinner, you will continue to sin. But that is what you *used to* be; that is not what you are anymore, if you've received Christ. If Christ lives in you, wherever you go, he goes.

Ephesians 3:19-20 says it perfectly:

[That you may really come] to know [practically, through experience for yourselves] the love of Christ, which far surpasses mere knowledge [without experience]; that you may be filled [through all your being] unto all the fullness of God [may have the richest measure of the divine Presence, and become a body wholly filled and flooded with God Himself]!

Now to Him Who, by (in consequence of) the [action of His] power that is at work within us, is able to [carry out His purpose and] do superabundantly, far over and above all that we [dare] ask or think [infinitely beyond our highest prayers, desires, thoughts, hopes, or dreams]. (AMP)

With Christ, you become a body *flooded* with God.

And with God in us, we can do anything.

That, my friends, is some pretty powerful stuff.

Jesus Power

Here's the thing you have to understand. It is not you or your power that is resisting the Enemy; it is Christ in you resisting the Enemy.

How exactly does that work?

Well, for example, back at my old church, every Sunday morning we had big crowds coming in, so there was a police officer out in front of the church directing traffic. Occasionally, you would see him put his hand out to the car that was coming his way, and all of a sudden the car would come to a stop. Now, did that car stop because the officer had super powers? No! It wasn't about the police officer's power; it was the power of his authority.

My pastor used to say that the police officer understood something: He knew that the City of Edmond, Oklahoma, was behind him. They backed him with the City of Edmond's authority, and he had the right to stop any traffic coming toward him at any time. It was not his power or his authority but the authority of the city that stopped that car.

Unbelievable as it may seem, you and I have been given an authority even greater than the City of Edmond, Oklahoma; we have been given the authority and power of God through Jesus Christ. Remember, the same power that raised Christ from the dead is alive in you and me.

Luke 10:19, in the Amplified Bible, says it like this: "Behold! I have given you authority and power to trample upon serpents and scorpions, and [physical and mental strength and ability] over all the power that the enemy [possesses]; and nothing shall in any way harm you."

It doesn't get much more powerful than that, does it? And that power lives in you.

The power that created the universe, the power that split the Red Sea, the power that raised Jesus Christ after three days— *that power* is inside of you.

Power in Action

The Bible says that God is the head and we are the body (see Ephesians 1:22-23). So what does that mean? Well, I believe that it means something different for the church as a whole, but in my own life, I think of it this way: If my head tells me that I want a drink of water and the water is sitting right in front of me on the counter, my head can want all day long to get a drink of that water, but my body must be the one to perform the act that my head wants it to do.

LOVE

God is speaking to us through his Holy Spirit and telling us things that you and I need to do, but if you and I aren't listening to the head, we don't follow as the body. What God is telling us to do will never get done.

One of the most spiritual things any of us could do today isn't just go to church another Sunday or another Wednesday or go to a camp or retreat. All of those things are great, but one of the most spiritual things we could accomplish is to do something in the natural to make the supernatural happen.

In the natural world, Moses just stretched out his hand and put the staff in the water. But that was the catalyst that invited the supernatural power of God to split the Red Sea in a majestic display of power.

Another not-so-majestic example happened on the day I realized I could be free from pornography. I went to my college roommate and told him that I needed him to put a password on my computer. Once I had my roommate put a password on the computer, it was almost impossible for me to look at pornography. It was a natural, physical action that set in motion the healing power of God, and I've been free from that evil ever since.

Some of you say that you want to quit, but you aren't really taking the natural action to make it happen. God is asking you to do that. James 4:7 says, "Submit yourselves, then, to God. Resist the devil, and he will flee from you."

This verse does *not* say for you to come and pray to God and ask him to resist the Devil, does it?

Many times while I was having issues with pornography, I would pray, *God, oh God, please take this away.* How many of you have done this? Asking God to take something away was probably the biggest part of my prayer time with God. And the crazy thing is, it didn't work.

So then I'd ask, *God, God, oh God, why are you not taking this away? I'm asking you to take this feeling away, take this urge away, take this hindrance away from me, but it never works.*

Why? Go back and read James 4:7 again.

Resisting the Devil is something that *you* have to do.

You're the only one who can do it. It's your job.

Think about it: Some of you have an issue with pornography and you need to put a password on your computer. Some of you have an issue with cutting and hurting yourself and the first step for you is to put down the instrument you're using. You need to tell somebody. Get it out in the open and allow someone into your life and share what it is you're struggling with. You can actively resist the Devil that way. Some of you have an alcohol problem. Put down that drink and seek help. Steer clear of situations that involve drinking in the first place.

Some of you are in a relationship with a boy or girl or man or woman and you need to get out of that relationship today. Sometimes the most spiritual thing you can do is break off that relationship. No ring, no thing. Yes, you may have messed up in the past, or maybe you haven't. Regardless, from this point forward, you need to tell that boy or girl or man or woman, "Unless I have a ring on my finger, you ain't getting none of this thing."

Okay, it sounds funny, but I'm so very serious when I say that. God is not going to send a Facebook message to your boyfriend or girlfriend and break up with him or her. Some of you know that you need to get out of that relationship you're in — for whatever reason — but you're still choosing to stay in it because of the past that you have with that person. But no matter how hard you pray, God is not going to make the breakup happen; *you're* going to have to do it.

Whatever you do, you don't need to just be hiding it, praying for God to free you from it; you need to take action. Do something about it. Today.

When you do, I promise you this: You'll see the power of God follow.

Re-Re-Re-Resist

The thing you have to understand about resisting is that it isn't something you do just one time. In fact, you'll likely spend your entire life resisting evil.

Let's say that someone breaks into your home while you're watching your favorite reality show in your living room. They bust in your front door, grab your flat-screen TV, and start heading out your front door. You are not just going to say, "Hey, God, can you tell them to put that down? God, I just pray that the burglars who broke into my house will put down my amazing fifty-two-inch, flat-screen TV. Thank you." And you go to the other room to watch a different TV. Right?

No. You are going to jump up off the couch, put them in the full nelson, and hold them there until they give up. And if they got up again and grabbed your TV another time, you're going to continue to fight them and resist them until they leave or the cops come and take them away. That is exactly how you and I are supposed to treat sin in our lives. It is your job to resist and protect all of the godly things in your life. If that sin comes back again, you must resist repeatedly until that sin has completely surrendered to the Christ in you.

Walk in the Confidence of God

You see, Jesus is passing on the baton to us, and now—as crazy as it sounds—we are to walk in the same authority and power that Jesus did. Yes, Jesus was the Son of God, but he was also the Son of Man. You and I are also the daughters and sons of God.

It's not just about grabbing a ticket to heaven and then for the rest of our days acting helpless until Jesus comes back. Church isn't all about not sinning; it's also about truly living in power. And I think it's time for the men and women of God to truly stand up and start owning the authority that God has given them. It would make such an impact on our schools, families, and marriages.

God has already given that authority to us, and it is our job to walk in confidence of what we already have been given. If you understand that you have been given the authority over evil in every area of your life, I think you'll spend less time asking God for the authority and more time acting on the authority he has already given to you.

And that's when the Christian life becomes fun. It's so freeing to know that whatever I face today and whatever you face today, God has already (past tense!) given me and you everything we need to overcome the Enemy. And we have been given the permission and the authority to do so.

Food for the Road

When the Israelites were preparing for the first Passover—you know the story—they brushed lamb's blood over and on the sides of their doors. But the crazy thing about this story is that they normally burn the sacrifice. In this situation, however,

God instructed the Israelites to eat the meat of the lamb. Why? It's because he knew that their bodies needed nutrition for what was happening that next day.

Jesus knew the same thing about us. The lamb is a representation of Christ dying on the cross. Yes, his blood covers our sin so we can have a ticket to heaven, but it's not just that. In Acts 1:8, Jesus said he's sending the helper, the advocate, the Holy Spirit to live inside of us.

It's not about your strength or your abilities or your talents—it's about him. The Holy Spirit that now resides in you will give you everything you need today to live for godliness. Second Peter 1:3 reminds us, "His divine power has given us everything we need for a godly life through our knowledge of him who called us by his own glory and goodness." Christ promised you that you have everything you need today to live out what God has put in front of you.

It Is Finished

When Jesus cried out from the cross, "It is finished" (John 19:30), he wasn't saying that his job was halfway done, so you and I have to do the other half. When Jesus sat down on his throne, there was no more work to be done. He has already done it.

He has already overcome the addiction that you're facing. He has already overcome your cutting problem. He has already overcome bulimia, anorexia, homosexual thoughts and tendencies, alcoholism, sexual addiction, pornography, smoking, lust—anything that can be named, Jesus Christ has overcome it.

Jesus Christ's dying on the cross for us wasn't just for a destination; Jesus also left the earth so he could put his Spirit in us, to journey with us to our destination. And in empowering us and nourishing us, he has given us everything we need to finish the work he has started in us until the day Christ Jesus returns (see Philippians 1:6).

Right here, in this very moment, you have been given all of the Jesus you're ever going to need. If you have ever in your life received Jesus as your Savior, the ball is in your court. The choice is yours. So go, do right now what God is putting on your heart to do. And tomorrow, you can walk in freedom like you've never experienced before in your life. Jesus Christ has taken away every excuse we have.

The power is yours.

The authority is yours.

The choice is yours.

Tell the Truth

1. What have you been praying for God to take care of in your life?

2. What are some ways you can take natural action, today, to invite the supernatural power of God?

3. What are some ways, some habits, some patterns you can develop to make sure you continue walking in the truth and light of God?

Conclusion

WELL, GUYS AND gals, throughout this ugly journey of poop and porn and permed mullets, I hope you've learned one thing.

(And if you didn't, you can find it in John 8:32 in your instruction manual.)

"The truth will set you free."

It really is that simple.

It's so easy that even a first grader gets it.

1. When you're in a mess, don't just sit in it. Do something about it.
2. When the secretary or God—whichever the case may be—asks about your mess, tell the truth about your situation.
3. When help arrives, look up and know they love you no matter what.
4. Put on your clean underwear and renew your mind.
5. Repeat #4. Daily.

No matter what lies you are told or what kind of mess you're in, it doesn't change who you are—or whose you are.

You are God's. Christ died for you, and he lives in you.

That's all the truth you'll ever need to know.

Now go and walk in that truth.

Resources

The Bridge to Life

Step 1 — God's Love and His Plan

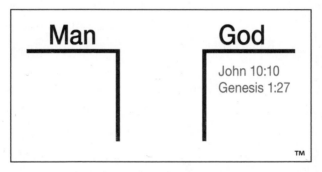

God created us in his own image to be his friend and to experience a full life assured of his love, abundant and eternal.

- Jesus said, "I have come that they may have life, and have it to the full." (John 10:10)
- We have peace with God through our Lord Jesus Christ. (Romans 5:1)

God planned for us to have peace and abundant life right now, so why are most people not having this experience?

Step 2 — Our Problem: Separation from God

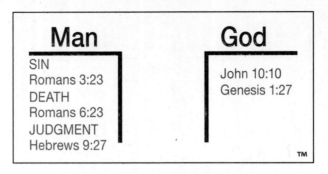

God created us in his own image to have abundant (meaningful) life. He did not make us robots to automatically love and obey him, but he gave us a will and freedom of choice. We chose to disobey God and go our own willful way. We still make this choice today. This results in separation from God.

- All have sinned and fall short of the glory of God. (Romans 3:23)
- Your iniquities have separated you from your God; your sins have hidden his face from you, so that he will not hear. (Isaiah 59:2)

On our own, there's no way we can attain the perfection needed to bridge the gap to God. Through the ages, individuals have tried many ways, without success. Good works won't do it (or religion or money or morality or philosophy).

- There is a way that appears to be right, but in the end it leads to death. (Proverbs 14:12)

Step 3 — God's Remedy: The Cross

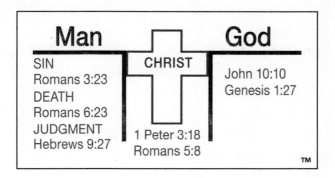

Jesus Christ is the only answer to this problem. He died on the cross and rose from the grave, paying the penalty for our sin and bridging the gap between God and people.

- Christ also suffered once for sins, the righteous for the unrighteous, to bring you to God. (1 Peter 3:18)
- There is one God and one mediator between God and mankind, the man Christ Jesus. (1 Timothy 2:5)
- God demonstrates his own love for us in this: While we were still sinners, Christ died for us. (Romans 5:8)

Step 4 — Our Response

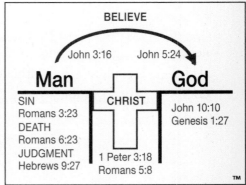

Believing means trust and commitment: acknowledging our sinfulness, trusting Christ's forgiveness, and letting him control our lives. Eternal, abundant life is a gift for us to receive.

- God so loved the world that he gave his one and only Son, that whoever believes in him shall not perish but have eternal life. (John 3:16)
- Very truly I tell you, whoever hears my word and believes him who sent me has eternal life and will not be judged but has crossed over from death to life. (John 5:24)

Is there any reason why you should not cross over to God's side and be certain of eternal life?

How to Receive Christ

1. Admit your need (that you are a sinner).
2. Be willing to turn from your sins (repent).
3. Believe that Jesus Christ died on the cross to pay the penalty for your sins and rose from the grave.
4. Through prayer, invite Jesus Christ to come in and control your life through the Holy Spirit (receive him as Lord and Savior of your life).

What to Pray

Dear Lord Jesus, I know I am a sinner and need your forgiveness. I know I deserve to be punished for my sins, and I believe that you died to pay that price and rose from the grave. I want to turn from my sins. I now invite you to come into my heart and life. I want to trust and follow you as the Lord and Savior of my life. Thank you for your forgiveness and the everlasting life I now have. Amen.

God's Assurance of Eternal Life

If you've prayed this prayer and are trusting Christ, the Bible says you can be sure you have eternal life.

- Everyone who calls on the name of the Lord will be saved. (Romans 10:13)
- It is by grace you have been saved, through faith—and this is not from yourselves, it is the gift of God—not by works, so that no one can boast. (Ephesians 2:8-9)
- Whoever has the Son has life; whoever does not have the Son of God does not have life. I write these things to you who believe in the name of the Son of God so that you may know that you have eternal life. (1 John 5:12-13)

Receiving Christ, we are born into God's family through the supernatural work of the Holy Spirit who indwells every believer. This is called regeneration, or the "new birth."

What Next?

This is just the beginning of a wonderful new life in Christ. To deepen this relationship, you should:

1. Maintain regular intake of the Bible to know Christ better.
2. Talk to God every day in prayer.
3. Tell others about your new faith in Christ.

4. Worship, live in community, and serve with other Christians in a church where Christ is preached.
5. As Christ's representative in a needy world, demonstrate your new life by your love and concern for others.[3]

Notes

1. Henry T. Blackaby and Richard Blackaby, *Experiencing God Day-by-Day: The Devotional and Journal* (Nashville: Broadman, Holman, 1997), 220.
2. Blackaby and Blackaby, 220.
3. The Navigators, "The Bridge to Life," 2011, www.navigators.org/us/resources/illustrations/items/ The%20Bridge%20to%20Life.

Author

KETRIC NEWELL literally burst into the world and onto the ministry scene with a vivacity that is truly God-given. From first to third grade, Ketric's teachers thought he had a hearing problem because he was so loud; it turned out that Ketric was just overloaded with energy and expression! Ketric was diag-

nosed with a reading disability later in his childhood, but he didn't let that stop him. In a Moses kind of way, God showed Ketric how he could have an awesome impact on the people around him *because* of the disability he wanted to hide.

For five years, Ketric served as youth pastor at LifeChurch .tv in Edmond, Oklahoma, working with more than four hundred students a week. Ketric and his wife, Ashley, and their two dogs recently moved to Nashville, Tennessee, where Ketric is a youth pastor at CrossPoint.tv.

Ketric first picked up the Bible at age thirteen, and it was the first book he'd ever read and actually understood! From there, Ketric attended weekly Bible studies, and without ever hearing the passages analyzed before, he stood up and spoke about what he thought the verses meant. Soon after, Ketric was asked by teachers and leaders to speak in front of various audiences.

Ketric's work in the Christian church really launched after taking care of his father, who had been diagnosed with cancer. After assisting his father for eight months, Ketric visited LifeChurch.tv and was asked to become a youth pastor. He called home for support from his parents and during that phone call, he learned that his mother had recently accepted Christ in her life. Soon after, his father was healed from his cancer.

Ketric loves speaking to young people and twenty-somethings at retreats and camps. Even though he's still in his twenties, Ketric has a strong passion for ministering to men and women of all ages.